MA5

1st UK

SWEEP SEARCH

SWEEP SEARCH

Hamish MacInnes

HODDER AND STOUGHTON
LONDON SYDNEY AUCKLAND TORONTO

British Library Cataloguing in Publication Data
MacInnes, Hamish
   Sweep search.
   1. Mountaineering—Scotland—Accidents and injuries
   I. Title
   363.1'4   GV200.183

   ISBN 0 340 37258 3

Hodder and Stoughton Editorial Office: 47 Bedford Square, London WC1B 3DP.

CONTENTS

ILLUSTRATIONS

CREDITS

Asterisked photographs by Alan Thomson. All others by
Hamish MacInnes.

SALUTE

I would like to thank all who helped with the compilation of this book. Without the assistance of Glencoe Mountain Rescue Team members, several of the casualties, RAF helicopter personnel and Police, both active and retired, these stories could never have been written.

The above and others dug deep into their memories, patience and time to enable me to put together these accounts of rescues as accurately as possible. It is these individuals whose role, like that of the Unknown Soldier, is often unsung. They are the heroes of mountain rescue; not just in Glencoe, but everywhere where there are mountains and climbers to fall off them.

Lastly, I'm indebted to Betsy Brantley for weeding irrelevancies from the text, as well as for her constructive criticism.

HAMISH MACINNES
GLENCOE 1985

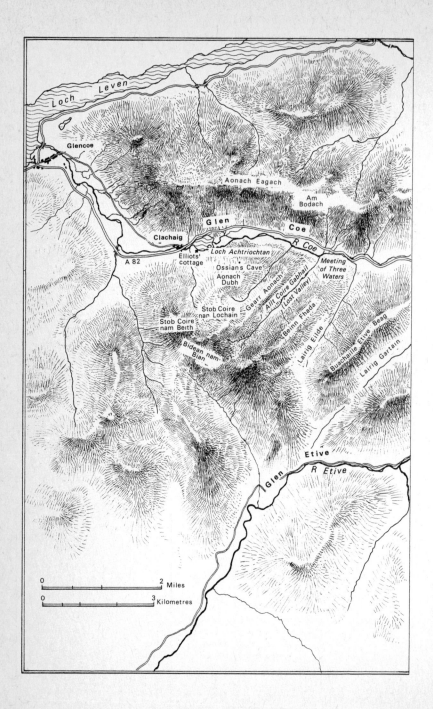

Loch Leven

Glencoe

Aonach Eagach

Am Bodach

Glen Coe

R Coe

Clachaig

A 82

Elliots' cottage

Loch Achtriochtan

Meeting of Three Waters

Ossian's Cave

Aonach Dubh

Gearr Aonach

Allt Coire Gabhail (Lost Valley)

Stob Coire nan Lochain

Stob Coire nam Beith

Beinn Fhada

Lairig Eilde

Buachaille Etive Beag

Lairig Gartain

Bidean nam Bian

Glen Etive

R Etive

0   2 Miles

0   3 Kilometres

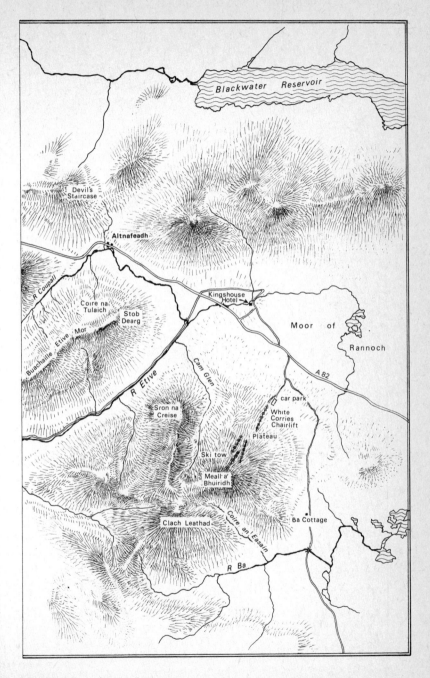

Blackwater Reservoir

Devil's Staircase

Altnafeadh

R Coupall

Coire na Tulaich

Stob Dearg

Buachaille · Etive · Mor

Kingshouse Hotel

Moor of

Rannoch

R Etive

Cam Glen

A 82

Sron na Creise

car park

White Corries Chairlift

Plateau

Ski tow

Meall· a' Bhuiridh

Clach Leathad

Coire an Easain

Ba Cottage

R Ba

1

THE TEAM AND THE GLEN

Some of the stories in this book involve serious injury and even death. Be that as it may, I don't look on death from either a morbid or callous viewpoint. Those mountaineers who died climbing did so pursuing the sport that they loved. All who climb or participate in any sport with an element of danger must accept the possibility of this ultimate penalty. There is often, I must admit, an attitude of 'it can't happen to me', but deep down we all know that it can and that it occasionally does.

There would have been no point in writing this book if it contained only lived-happily-ever-after tales. Some of them are, but the book represents a cross-section of rescues; all are true and have been checked by members of the team, as well as by some of the survivors.

The events are recorded simply and without trimmings as I, my fellow rescuers, and the rescued saw them and I hope that this account will give some insight into the mountain rescue scene, not just in Glencoe, but all over Britain, for our local team is just one of many who go out in all weathers at any time of the day or night, often out of pocket, frequently out of puff, to help our fellow climbers. Not because we are jolly good chaps, but because we like doing it. Rescue keeps us fit, gives us something to talk about and bestows on us the selfish satisfaction of feeling that we are doing good.

Glencoe is probably best known for three things: its Massacre, its rain and its mountains. Perhaps not in that order if you happen to be a climber, a meteorologist or a Campbell. The glen runs approximately east and west, about halfway up the ragged coastline of Western Scotland, some eighteen miles from Fort William and eighty-five miles from Glasgow via the 'high road' along the bonnie banks of Loch Lomond. I came to live in this rocky defile in 1958, but prior to that I was a dedicated and frequent visitor. There is an old Hindu saying, 'He who goes to the hills, goes to his mother.' Glencoe certainly has been a long-suffering foster mother to me.

The area has always been a popular one for mountaineers and with this popularity came the inevitable mishaps, some minor, some serious. But up until 1962 there was no official rescue team in the glen, just a few dedicated shepherds and the village bobby to carry down the injured from the crags. In those days mountain rescue was, as indeed it is now, often centred on the Elliots' home. For years Mr Elliot was in the forefront of Glencoe rescue, a Samaritan to those who fell by the wayside, or rather the mountainside. Rustling up a few fellow farmers and shepherds, he would set off with his shepherd's crook, a kerosene storm lantern, some faith, and a lot of charity.

On one occasion, when sons Walter and Willie were mere lads, a climber came down from Bidean nam Bian. His friend had fallen. As there was no telephone at the Elliots' house to raise the alarm, the man borrowed Mr Elliot's bicycle and headed for Clachaig. His progress was probably fast, but certainly erratic. He almost had a head-on collision with 'Dodo' Cameron, a local gamekeeper, and both had to pick themselves up from the gravel track.

As Dodo said when he reached the Elliots' home a short time afterwards: "There's some madman oot there on a bike who almost killed me." To prove his point he produced a pedal, the pedal of Mr Elliot's bicycle. Never again did Mr Elliot loan his trusty steed, no matter how dire the emergency!

I had been on rescues in the glen before I actually came to live here. It was on a rescue that I made my first acquaintance with the Elliot family. In the autumn of 1955, I had completed a climb on Bidean nam Bian with John Cunningham, a great friend of mine. We were coming off the hill when we saw a figure striding across the rough ground just above the small whitewashed Elliot cottage beside Loch Achtriochtan. It was Willie, one of the sons. He asked if we could help take a chap out of the Chasm, a climb on Buachaille Etive Mor. The casualty had been attempting the route with his son and had broken a leg. The evacuation didn't cause us many problems, only a lot of hard work, for there were only five of us, plus the local bobby in his wellingtons. That rescue in 1955 with the Elliot brothers proved to be the first of hundreds on which we took part together.

Over a period of some three score years there are many tales which involve that little innocent-looking white cottage. It has been used as a temporary mortuary on occasions and there was even an incident in which a man, and a Campbell to boot, rose from the dead after having fallen off Church Door Buttress on Bidean nam Bian in blizzard conditions. He was given up for dead and deposited in a spare room for collection, but somehow he revived, much to everyone's surprise. Many years later he read an account of his accident in my earlier book, *Call-Out*, and visited the Elliot family to pay his respects, clutching that esteemed Highland plenipotentiary, a bottle of malt whisky.

Another vital member of the Elliot family is Doris. Like her mother before her, Doris has for years been instrumental in calling out the team and tending the often shocked and injured survivors who stagger down to announce some fresh calamity on the hills at the back door of the cottage. On one occasion recently she got closer to the business end of a rescue than she'd bargained for.

It started when a girl fell on the Aonach Eagach Ridge, the northern three-mile-long, 3000-foot-high bastion of the glen. The south face of the ridge rising up from the A82 is very steep, riven by gullies and grotty buttresses. It was summer, but a dark and drizzly night. As you read this book you will realise that there is seldom daylight, fair weather or a convenient time when we are called out.

Will Thomson was the first of our team to set off. A helicopter had been requested, but you can't be sure that it will materialise after dark. Will decided to take a route which would lead him up beside a line of steep and in places overhanging cliffs. He thought that it was above this that he had seen the light of the injured girl, but it was difficult to tell in the dark on such a vast expanse of mountainside. The rest of the team following decided to go further right of Will's route.

After about forty minutes, Will was well up the side of the escarpment. Ian Nicholson (who was suffering from flu), Davy Gunn and other team members thought that Will was too far left and Ian shouted to him.

"Hey, Will, you'd better come over this way, she's over to your right."

"That's bloody funny," Will yelled back, "for I'm with her now."

Despite the initial doubt, an RAF helicopter did arrive. It wasn't a Wessex from Leuchars in Fife which usually serves our area, but a Sea King from Lossiemouth, which is a larger aircraft with night-flying capability. But after a lot of trouble, due to darkness and rain, it had to give up trying to get near the casualty and the team started down, carrying the girl on the stretcher. Meanwhile the Sea King put down on the field in front of the Elliots' house, illuminated by the dipped headlights of the Police Range Rover. After an hour or so the pilot decided to have another go at uplifting the casualty, but once more had to retreat through the black void to what he thought was the light from the Range Rover. The fine drizzle of rain had now turned to a proper downpour. As the large machine approached the lights, visibility was desperate. Doris and her sister Ray were observing the operation from the front door – what they could see of it. They watched the lights of the fat noisy machine descending towards earth. This is Doris's recollection of the scene: "Instead of touching down in the field, the helicopter came closer and closer and closer. The noise was deafening. By this time it was very low and when it was only a few feet away from us, Ray and I took off. I glanced through the wee window in the porch as I scuttled along the corridor and saw the huge landing wheels just above the door, almost on the guttering. The tail was between Walter's van and the side of the house and gravel was whipped up and splattered against the walls and windows. Ray and I dashed for the door into the living room and nearly got jammed in it in our panic."

Inside, Alec McEwan, Doris's brother-in-law, and his son, Sandy, were peering in disbelief out of the window. Alec shouted, "Where did he go?"

The pilot realised at the last moment that it wasn't the lights of the Range Rover he was heading for, but the one-storey cottage. The Police Range Rover had been called away a short time before the Sea King came back in. Hence the error. It was a miracle that the helicopter's rotors didn't decapitate the chimneys or the television aerial, not to mention a nearby rowan tree.

Though I made Glencoe my home as from 1958, it wasn't until 1962 that we got down to the business of forming a rescue team. The reason for this formality was that it's easier to obtain funds for an official-sounding body. So one evening, in the lounge of the Clachaig Inn over a few pints, several of us got together for the first meeting of the Glencoe Mountain Rescue Association. Of the founder members, only Denis Barclay, Walter and Willie Elliot and myself are still rescue active. Rescuers have come and gone here over the years. Several of them have met their end in the mountains, both here and in the Himalayas, while others have quietly hung up their rucsacks, content that over the years they've done their best to help their fellow climbers in times of need.

After a few months of fund-raising, we managed to purchase several pairs of boots and a couple of ropes. Denis and I were the only two who did any 'proper' climbing. The rest of the team were farmers, or shepherds like the Elliot brothers. However, in those early days we could call upon the considerable talents of Bill Smith and Harry MacKay, both of the Creagh Dhu Mountaineering Club, then working with Denis Barclay at the White Corries chairlift. By the time the team was formed, they had moved to Aviemore as the robust backbone of the then infant Cairngorm Chairlift Company. Bill Smith and John Cunningham were then Scotland's most talented climbers, and I spent many happy days in their company, here, in New Zealand and, with John, in the Himalayas. The Glencoe Mountain Rescue Association was officially recognised by the Mountain Rescue Committee, the national body, and also enjoyed the blessing of the Argyll County Police. The Chief Constable, Kenneth MacKinnon, proved to be a long-suffering ally of our renegade group, and assisted us in many ways.

Since climbers first started to fall off Scottish mountains, the Police have had an interest in mountain rescue. Many a Highland bobby whose beat took in the high tops sallied forth like that Glencoe constable, usually wearing wellie boots and armed with more resolution than know-how. Kenneth MacKinnon was probably the first Chief Constable in Scotland to interpret the Police Code and its 'protection of life and property' clause as a commission for his force to take a more positive part in evacuating the injured from the hills. He felt it was a statutory duty and suggested that our team should enrol as special constables. We went along with it at first, as we thought we could get equipment more easily that way. However, the scheme just didn't work, and we soon found ourselves floundering in red tape. It said a lot for Kenneth MacKinnon's magnanimity that, when we resigned from the ranks, he held no grudge and remained our staunch supporter.

One obvious reason for Police concern over mountain accidents is the possibility of foul play. Provided you can get your victim to a convenient drop and have the energy and the ill-will to shove, there is no easier way to perpetrate a crime. It has, in fact, been done on occasion. One, in recent years, was quite blatant. A couple from the continent were staying in Edinburgh for their honeymoon. When doing a tour of the Scottish capital the brand-new husband pushed his newly insured wife to her death over Salisbury Crags, close to Holyrood Palace.

Today the Police are getting more involved in rescue, with some areas assigned their own mountain rescue teams. This, in my opinion, is a retrograde step. Like mountaineering, rescue is a specialised task. One has to be an able climber to be a competent rescuer, used to the hills and able to be on the spot to give immediate first-aid to the injured in the shortest possible time. In other words, local teams with a nucleus of mountaineers, backed by helicopters and the Police, are the ideal mountain rescue arrangement. Our own experience in Glencoe convinced me of this.

We were fortunate until his recent retirement to have Mr Donald Henderson as Chief Constable of the Highland Region. He was aware of these fundamental criteria of speed and efficiency in this life or death matter. With our combined efforts those who fall victim to the Scottish mountains have never had it so good.

In Scotland, the rescuer is insured through the local Police authority. The Highland Region seems to have the 'most valuable animals' if compensation is anything to go by, but some teams also invest in separate insurance of their own. A further policy covers helicopter rescue, which includes winching operations.

This book slightly overlaps the timespan of *Call-Out*, my last account of Glencoe rescues. I have included one or two earlier incidents to give perspective to the change that has taken place over the past few years from the sweat-and-toil era to the whisk-away service of today's helicopters. This transition has come about with the advent of the Wessex helicopter, and later the Sea King. These two aircraft, operated by the RAF, have proved worthy workhorses in the most appalling conditions, be it blizzard, darkness, deluge or storm.

Prior to this, the Whirlwind served us on many occasions. It didn't have the power or the reliability of its younger brothers, though I can remember call-outs when we were more than glad to see this ungainly beast come to our aid. On one particular scramble the pilot was John Stirling, who had a long association with the team. John was something akin to the gentlemen aces of World War One and had a swashbuckling style to match. He was a Sir Galahad of the air who used to materialise out of the sky in his shining yellow armour. On this particular day, a climber had fallen from Jericho Wall, the crux pitch in Clachaig Gully, a long and somewhat vegetated climb. Davy Gunn, a local lad, came up with me. Davy was a newcomer to the team, and has since become a dedicated rock climber. After going halfway up the side of the gully on the true right bank we cut into it and soloed up the pitches to Jericho Wall. With the help of a couple of casual climbers, we lowered the injured man on a rope cableway to the bottom of the Great Cave pitch, a stumbling block on the early attempts to scale Clachaig Gully. The casualty wasn't badly injured, having broken a wrist and nose, but he was too shocked to walk. So we were very pleased to see John's Whirlwind coming to our assistance at that very moment. The injured man was winched aboard and whisked off to hospital in Fort William.

By the time we got back to the main road, two other

accidents had taken place. I managed to get a call through to Fort William Police to ask for John's help once more. In those days, we didn't have any direct communication with the helicopters ourselves, so we couldn't give John an exact location. When the aircraft came low up the glen, he spotted us by the side of the road. There was no convenient place to put the large machine down, so, without hesitation, he landed alongside our vehicles, in the middle of the A82 highway and effectively blocked the road. Two queues of cars quickly formed on either side of the helicopter, as it was at the height of the tourist season. The next customer in the rescue queue was a man who had broken his leg on the northern slopes of Aonach Dubh. After he was taken down, the last client of the day was dealt with, a girl who was exposed high on the Aonach Eagach Ridge and who, it transpired, was not in dire need of our services.

Accounts of call-outs, by their very nature, are stories of disaster. But to the rescue team there are always light-hearted moments, even in the most heart-rending situations. A typical example took place a few years ago when we were out searching for a German student who had plunged to his death on an ice-bound peak. Shepherds have an intimate knowledge of their patch, knowing the easiest and safest way off the tops – the way they gather the sheep. On this parti-cular call-out I asked the local shepherd if he could come along with us, as the climbing wasn't too technical and his know-how, especially in the dark, would be invaluable. I wasn't immediately aware that he was very much under the weather, though I should have detected the overpowering smell of a popular blended whisky. Just before setting off, I gave him one of our walkie-talkies so that he could keep in contact with us. My enlightenment in respect of his sobriety came with the voice of his wife, loud and clear over our radios. He had gone back into his house with the walkie-talkie inadvertently switched on.

"Yer no gang up the hill in that drunken state, ye stupid

auld bugger, an' yer no takking that other half-bottle wi
ye . . ."

I don't know if he managed to get the half-bottle or not,
but he came with us. Even now I can recollect him sliding
out of control down steep snow in his upturned Herd-laddie
boots. I yelled to him, "Get your stick in, man, or you'll kill
yourself." He grasped his shepherd's crook and was now
sober enough to take the necessary preventative measures
and save himself.

Rescue from the hills and mountains of Britain is free to
the unfortunate who get into trouble. Overseas the rescued
don't fare so well, certainly not financially. In many countries rescue is a service which must be paid for in hard cash.
Nowadays, our local teams are backed up by rescue helicopters, usually from the RAF. This service is free by courtesy
of the Ministry of Defence. As well as fulfilling a humanita-
rian need, it provides training for the crews who will have to
fly regularly in hazardous conditions. The RAF have mountain rescue teams, too. Their primary function is to search
for crashed aircraft, but they also assist, mainly on searches
or protracted rescues where extra manpower is required.
Until about fifteen years ago they played a very important
role in outlying areas where rescue teams hadn't been established.

Today virtually every mountain or moorland area in
Britain has its own rescue group and in some regions they
are more prolific than their potential customers. In the
Highlands of Scotland they have to cover a vast area in
higher mountains, and evacuations can be long and com-
plicated. Volunteer groups like the Glencoe team are drawn
from all walks of life. Many are climbers, but not exclusively
so. In the more remote areas the majority of volunteers are
shepherds, forestry workers and farmers.

There is often a general lack of public sympathy for the
mountain accident victim and rescue teams sometimes have
difficulty raising cash to equip their members. As well as

devoting a large percentage of their free and sometimes working hours to helping the injured, they have the onerous task of running dances and raffles to pay for their own boots. Funds were always desperately low in the early days and sometimes we couldn't even afford batteries for our headlamps.

Avalanches are still the greatest source of danger that confronts a Scottish rescue team. In recent years there has been a tremendous upsurge in winter climbing and each winter more and more mountaineers come from overseas to climb in what are advertised as 'Arctic ice conditions'.

In fact, more often than not the mountains and gullies are wet and slushy – but possibly just as avalanche-prone. Though there hasn't been an increase over the years in avalanches, there has been a profound influx of winter mountaineers to share the annual snow slides. Apart from the use of helicopters, one of the most significant modern rescue aids is the avalanche bleeper, an instrument the size of a cigarette packet, which, when switched to transmit, emits a bleep every second or so. If a transmitter and wearer is buried in an avalanche he can be detected by searchers who switch their units to receive and home in on the buried person. This has made avalanche search a lot safer for rescuers in many countries.

We do have search and rescue dogs, of course, but a four-legged friend can't get everywhere a skilled climber can. Dogs are used in summer and winter, and a single dog can be as effective as dozens of rescuers. If everyone used bleepers the dogs could be retired, but to date in this country the bleepers are worn mainly by rescue personnel, when they remember to, and a few concerned cross-country skiers.

I have a particular interest in the development of rescue equipment and try to keep abreast of modern developments. Through the Leishman Research Laboratory, at my home in Glencoe, I get visits from mountain rescue teams from all over the world and we discuss items of mutual interest. Recently our team obtained very powerful military night-viewing equipment – image intensifiers – which enable us to see quite clearly in a night with perhaps just a handful of stars visible. Many new methods are being tried and tested in the search and rescue field. In some parts of the world computers are used to co-ordinate large search operations and helicopters can be fitted with thermal imagers, very sensitive infra-red detectors which can detect even the smallest source of heat. Microwaves can also be deployed to locate lost climbers and skiers.

To some all this may seem a long way from the freedom of the hills, more like Big Brother putting on climbing boots. But one must remember that things look a whole lot different when a leg is broken or a skull cracked and a blizzard imminent. Most rescue team members are enthusiastic about the crags themselves, but anything which makes a rescue operation easier, more efficient and more comfortable for the patient is welcome. We are not playing to Queensberry Rules where perhaps the use of a piton is considered unsporting or pulling on a rope immoral. With rescue anything goes as long as it helps the victim. It is a team 'sport', each team having its own strikers and full backs. The game is often one of life or death, sometimes with all the handicaps which nature can muster piled up against you. This is possibly what appeals to the rescuer – the uncertainty of it. How to get the patient back to base in relative comfort with the fewest moves; how to sustain life which is sometimes hanging by a thread; how best to deploy rescue tools in a given situation.

It is interesting to reflect on the attitudes of most mountain rescue personnel towards those they rescue which contrasts markedly with that of the public at large. Admittedly, on occasion, we salvage some idiot in dire straits of his own making and one's patience is tried. A few years ago we went to the summit of Aonach Dubh to rescue a solo climber who had prearranged with his friends to use his electronic camera flash should he require the services of the team. When we reached him we discovered he was only suffering from cramp. But we persuaded him to walk down, possibly faster than he had ever done before. Recently we evacuated a climber who had fallen down the head of the Lost Valley in icy conditions. Though only bruised, he claimed he couldn't walk beyond the valley floor. One of our team, Denis Barclay, slipped on ice en route to the casualty, but managed to get back to base on his own with a broken ankle. Our stretcher case wasn't admitted by the hospital and was seen back on the Glencoe hills the next day.

But this doesn't happen very often. Usually injuries are genuine enough so, if incurred as the result of the climber's own folly, the lesson has already been spelt out in no uncertain manner by pain and discomfort, and anything we might add to those two powerful chastisements is superfluous. In our local team we make a point of not criticising the rescued. In any case, most of us are climbers ourselves and accidents do happen.

The British have always been a sporting nation and a voluntary service is a fine concept in this age of professionalism in sport. After all, rescuers are volunteers. They don't have to go out if they don't want to. Though there is no great risk in walking the fells and bens in summer, in winter the scene changes and verdant or heather-blooming hillsides can become death slides under hard snow and ice. But the young should be encouraged to partake in outdoor activities, including mountaineering, and with proper supervision can enjoy a rewarding and long-lasting pursuit. However, until they are experienced enough to look after themselves, they should be chaperoned by experts, especially on our higher snow-clad hills.

In this age when we are labelled and classified on some hard or floppy disk, it is important to get away from it all in the hills or on the sea. The luxury of solitude can still be found. One doesn't necessarily have to spend forty days and forty nights in the wilderness of your choice to put the jumble of life back into perspective but, while we recharge our batteries, we must also accept the attendant risk element.

2

WITH DOGS TO THE NORTH

Strange stories concerning missing walkers and climbers occur all the time. Some five years ago, I had a call from a man in Glasgow concerned that a friend who had just withdrawn from drugs had disappeared. The missing man had stated previously, in a depressed condition, that he intended to end his life in the Scottish mountains he loved so much, and my caller had discovered he had bought a single rail ticket to Crianlarich, a village about thirty-six miles from Glencoe.

I had to tell him it was outwith our search and rescue area, but he should contact the Central Region Police. Failing this (for there wasn't much evidence to justify searching such a vast mountain area) he could himself go to Crianlarich and question the station staff. It was October, a quiet month for tourists, and they would probably remember any solitary, non-local passenger.

I forgot all about the incident until recently when a skeleton was found by a shepherd at 2000 feet on Ben Odhair, north of Tyndrum, a short distance from Crianlarich. As far as could be ascertained, the body had been lying there for three or four years, about the time I had that odd 'phone call. I have no idea who it was that telephoned me, and to date the Police have failed to identify the body. Could there be some connection, I wonder?

A rather bizarre and unsolved case is that of a skeleton found in 1938 in Loch Avon, a remote loch in the heart of the Cairngorms. It was still dressed in the remains of a black suit. Close by were a walking stick and a brown leather attaché case. Within the case were pyjama trousers, a toilet roll, two collars, a pair of scissors, a box of matches and a handbill describing Simpson's Two-Day Tours. Nearby on a rock were a razor, shaving brush, comb, soap, toothpaste and a bowler hat. I have often speculated on the origin of Simpson's Two-Day Tours. Were these one-way – two-day – do-it-yourself tickets to oblivion? It is hard to imagine how anyone so dressed would contemplate making his way into this desolate region.

The story of the solitary hill walker, George Mack, is equally inconclusive, but I include it here because it illustrates the early days, and provides a link between the sort of mountain rescue I described in my earlier book, *Call-Out*, and the rescue scene today with its bleepers and its advances in helicopter capability. It is also a story from outside Glencoe. In the 1960s there were far fewer rescue groups in the further-flung corners of the Highlands and I was frequently called north to help out by the Police.

Early July of 1967 brought a spell of glorious weather to the Highlands. The midges hadn't started their summer campaign of harassment, but the tourist invasion was swelling to yet another record high. On the 8th of the month I received a telephone call from Sergeant Donnie Smith of what was then the Ross and Sutherland Constabulary. This was before the formation of the Northern Constabulary, whose jurisdiction is the whole of the north of Scotland and the Islands. Donnie, a stockily built chap with boundless enthusiasm, has a passion for map-reading and had taken on the task of co-ordinating a Police team for mountain rescue work.

"Hello, Hamish, are you busy?" I recognised his opening gambit.

"Well . . ." I began, but before I could finish, he continued, "We have a man missing on Ben More Assynt massif." He pronounced it 'masseeve'. "We could do with the rescue dogs."

"I doubt if I can rustle up any dogs other than my own at present, Donnie," I answered cautiously. "Nearly all the handlers are away on holiday just now. But," I added, "I could come up with our two, Rangi and Tiki, if that's any use?"

"That'll be just dandy," he responded. "We can pick you up in a patrol car at the county boundary."

"No thanks, Donnie. We'll take the Mini, it's cheap to run."

In those days there was no reimbursement for travelling expenses outside the respective Police regions so that volunteering to assist on rescues and searches usually meant I was out of pocket into the bargain.

"When will you be up, Hamish?"

"First thing in the morning."

"OK. I'll look forward to seeing you then."

There was something about this way-out Police force that I found fascinating. I got to know them well as I used to run their training for mountaineering and rescue, sometimes helped out by Dr Tom Patey, a brilliant mountaineer, who had a practice in Ullapool. I normally stayed with Tom when using Ullapool as a base, while the Police lodged in a local hostel which suited them fine. Conscientiously, like staunch upholders of law and order, they would rise with due cere- mony from the bar at 10.00 p.m. which was the official closing hour, and leave the premises, only to walk round the building and re-enter by the back door. Their carousing extended far into the night.

On one occasion, they were scheduled to give a demon- stration of their prowess as rescuers. It was the last day of a course and their Chief Constable, Mr Kenneth Ross, arrived, complete with the Police Committee, to observe a stretcher lower from a crag close to the road. However the last night for my pupils had finished at first light in the bar, and it was a sorry group of survivors which staggered up the hill that day, each one a potential candidate for the stretcher they were carrying. A rather generously propor- tioned spokesman of the Police Committee lumbered up to me and ominously cleared his throat.

"Meester MacInnes," he said accusingly, with a strong emphasis on the 'meester'. "I don't think that you should be giving these men such a strenuous training programme. They are obviously exhausted."

Quick to seize on this let-out, I agreed and suggested a modified exercise where I could keep the team away from the cliff and the possibility of a real-life evacuation!

In the small communities in north and west Scotland, the village bobby must be accepted as a local, otherwise his task would be impossible. He establishes a rapport with the people, yet still contrives in a quiet way to administer the law, interpreting it in a humane and just way, if not always according to the book. This is the secret of an efficient Police force in the Scottish outback, and visitors from the south and overseas never cease to be amazed at the understanding which exists between the Highlander and the 'fuzz'. Very often it is a case of poacher turned gamekeeper.

The next morning, with Dr Catherine MacInnes, who was then my wife, I drove up to Police headquarters at Dingwall. It was a sombre building, looking as if it had seen the shedding of many tears – it probably had, having formerly been a prison. Even then manacles were attached to the walls in its dank bowels which were subject to flooding by the North Sea. Obviously not the ideal place for arthritic internees. In a room boasting a door which could have served a fall-out shelter, I was briefed on what had happened to date in the search for the missing man, George Mack.

"He's forty years old," Donnie told me as he twiddled a pencil on his desk top, "and the only son of his widowed mother. Looks as if he was an experienced hillman, Hamish. Bit of a Munro bagger." A Munro is a peak over 3000 feet. "And he's done a fair amount abroad as well."

Before leaving Inchnadamph Hotel, Mack had left a very

detailed itinerary in his room. That was at 10.45 a.m. on the morning of the 8th. Donnie traced a line with his pencil over the map spread out on the top of his desk. "He intended to traverse Beinn Uidhe, Conival and Ben More Assynt and return to Inchnadamph for 7.00 p.m. We were informed when he didn't turn up for dinner."

"What was the weather like, Donnie?"

"A bit crappy, cloud on the tops, windy and heavy showers."

"And what's been done to date?"

"Our team went up there at 10.00 p.m. ready to start a search at 4.00 a.m. this morning. Your friend, Tom Patey, went up from Ullapool on the initial search, but he's back in Ullapool now. Also, Alan Jeffreys, that policeman potholer from Edinburgh, and one of his mates, Brian Reid, will be staying with Tom tonight. They're searching the caves now. I couldn't go up to join them as I've buggered my knee at rugby so I'm left here minding the long field. Oh, and Charlie Rhoden has asked the RAF mountain rescue boys at Kinloss to stand by."

Taking leave of Donnie, we started up the Ullapool road to the west coast, then continued northwards to the small cluster of houses which constitutes Elphin. This is wild and beautiful country, to my mind some of the finest anywhere on earth.

The old schoolhouse was being used as a base of operations by the Police. Inspector Charlie Rhoden, Donnie's boss, came out to meet us. Charlie is a tall, good-natured man, always willing to do a good turn, with a habit of rubbing his chin which he was doing as he greeted us.

"I'm glad you could make it, Hamish. It looks a difficult one . . . so much ground." A sweeping gesture of his arm indicated the surrounding hills. "Come on in and have a cuppa. I'm chief cook and bottle-washer."

Over tea and digestive biscuits we discussed with Charlie

the area of highest priority to search with the dogs, then drove round to the head of Loch Assynt and the Inchnadamph Hotel. Parking the car in a lay-by, we set off by the valley immediately behind the hotel, Rangi and Tiki quartering the rough ground with avid enthusiasm. They always knew when a search was imminent from the equipment I used to pack into my rucsack. Harnesses, too, were symbols of work to them, so they knew they had to concentrate on the job in hand once these were put on.

This is a limestone region which means caves. On the way up the valley we passed the mouths of various potholes currently being checked out by the pothole rescue lads from Edinburgh. I remember thinking we would have needed cairn terriers or Jack Russells for that type of search, but I had every confidence in Alan Jeffreys and Brian Reid for sniffing out a missing person underground. And it seemed as though the search was going to be left in their hands. My dogs covered an amazing amount of ground as we rose high on the west flank of Ben More Assynt, but by late afternoon I was fairly convinced that George Mack wasn't on the surface of this search area.

I had formed the Search and Rescue Dog Association a year or so before, after being on an avalanche dog handlers' course in Switzerland. The training system we adopted in Britain, however, also involved summer searches. The dogs work mainly on air scent, so no item of clothing is required, though in certain countries they do use tracking dogs such as bloodhounds. Rangi and Tiki, my German shepherds, were both founder members of the Association, and excellent work dogs. A good dog can do the work of fifty searchers. Rangi is aggressive and possessive, Tiki, a bitch, gentle, dainty and instantly obedient. On one occasion I told her to "sit and stay" at the bottom of a climb, but due to difficulties the route took over six hours. When I got back to the base she was sitting exactly where I'd left her beside my rucsack, patiently waiting.

Both dogs were tiring by the end of the day as we made our way down the valley. An apparition appeared from a hole in the ground in front of us, dressed in a multi-ripped wet suit. Mephistopheles himself? No, Alan Jeffreys, shortly followed by Brian Reid dressed like the wandering minstrel, in shreds and patches with a generous allocation of mud. They too had drawn a blank. Later Alan told me how Mack's itinerary had suggested to them that his walk would take him round the caves of Traligill, so they searched this area first, working from the foot of Conival. Next they had checked Cuil Dubh Sink, which is a short climb down to water, then the Cnoc nan Uamh system, a 4000-foot-long cave which has three easy entrances. They had squirmed their way through most of these, including the spectacular Waterslide, to no avail. As well as this impressive list they had investigated a further five holes and caves in the Inchnadamph area.

The huge disc of the sun was dipping its toes into the eastern Atlantic, firing the sea a deep crimson and, closer by, Loch Assynt, now partly in shadow, looked like smoked glass. As I moved slowly over the rugged ground, I thought of Montrose, that super-soldier, who had been betrayed for a ransom of twenty thousand Scots pounds and 400 boils of stale meal. He had languished in the confines of Ardvreck Castle on the shores of Loch Assynt before terminating his earthly campaign at the end of a rope in Edinburgh's Grassmarket.

Back at the schoolhouse that night, we sat, replete after a meal that demonstrated how well a Police Inspector's lot embraces the culinary arts. With the Police team back from their own day on the hills, we talked about where next to concentrate our search and the possibilities of finding George Mack alive.

Our conversation round the stove was interrupted by the roar of military vehicles. It was the RAF rescue team from Kinloss, near Inverness. John Hinde was in charge. John, big in both heart and stature, was a veteran of countless rescues and we had shared many a stretcher carry together. I went out to greet him.

"Hi, John," I shouted as the engines were cut. "Better late than never . . ."

"Better late than dead on time!" was the rejoinder from one of his lads.

"Hello, Hamish, any luck?" John called in his surprisingly quiet voice.

"Nope, not a sausage . . . You'd better have a word with the Inspector. He's inside."

The lingering, never-go-to-bed sky was still bright behind the fang of Suilven, Pillar Mountain, once a landmark to the Vikings who knew the area as Sudrland, the South Land, now Sutherland. We headed over to the Police rescue truck to snatch a few hours' shut-eye, for the schoolhouse was chock-a-block. The next thing I remember saying, while still half-asleep, was, "Yes, John, we must get on with this ruddy film . . ." I have no idea what I was thinking about, but it may have been connected with the first live TV outside-broadcast climb on the Old Man of Hoy which I had done a short time before. When I came to, John Hinde was looming above me like a totem pole.

"What's this film we're supposed to be doing, Hamish?" he asked with a laugh. "I woke you because we have just had a message via our radio truck from Rescue Control in Pitreavie. It's about another possible call-out in Torridon. Charlie Rhoden is away to telephone about it now."

"Well," I said, glancing at my watch with resignation, "it's quarter to four. Time all civilised rescuers showed a leg."

Just then Charlie looked into the truck. "It seems as if there's trouble in Torridon, lads," he said apologetically, rubbing his hand over his chin. "A couple of hill walkers thought they heard cries for help high on Liathach. For some reason known only to themselves, the boys didn't bother to report it. It was the driver of that wee bus that goes to Diabeg who raised the alarm. He heard them chatting about the calls. He made them telephone the Police station at Kinlochewe."

"Anything further?" I asked.

"Yes, the policeman at Kinlochewe – you know 'Splitpin', don't you? – went down the road and found a Ford van parked by the roadside directly under where the two boys heard the shouts. That's at the east end of the mountain directly up from the road."

"It doesn't look good," I said slowly, thinking about the treacherous Liathach sandstone terraces. After years of rescue work one gets a sixth sense for danger. This one had all the ingredients. John was of a similar opinion.

"I'll go immediately," I decided. "He could still be alive."

"Right, I'll follow with some of my lads," John said. "But I had better leave most of them here, to continue this search."

"Well, I suppose we'll manage all right." The Inspector spoke resignedly, obviously unhappy to lose searchers. "However, now that I think of it, I've quite a few reinforcements coming: RAF Leuchars, the Dounreay Atomic Power Station team and the Royal Navy, Arbroath. Besides that, I've about twenty-four Police officers and thirty local volunteers, plus the rescue helicopters. I think we'll get by."

"And the Lossiemouth Naval crowd told me that they would be here by six this morning," John added.

"Yes, yes, that will be fine," Charlie said. "I'll go and whistle up breakfast for you."

"Thanks, Charlie, you've taken up the wrong vocation; you could have made a fortune as a chef."

Catherine and I made fast time to Garve, which comprises a road junction, a hotel, a railway station and damn little

else. It looks as if God dumped it there in retribution for
some early sin. From Garve a road snakes west to the wild
and beautiful country of Achnashellach, Torridon and Loch
Maree.

There was little traffic on what was then a car's width
ribbon of tarmac, punctuated by the odd lay-by. As I accel-
erated up the hill and entered the mouth of the wide strath,
we saw a train. It must have been an early-morning goods
train going to Kyle of Lochalsh, obviously lightly laden
because it was belting along like the clappers. The driver
gave a friendly wave and a blast on his whistle, so I
responded with the Mini horn, which sounded more like the
belch of a eunuch: a quite inadequate means of heralding the
approach of this white tin box clawing its way flat out round
corners.

I don't think either the train driver or I intended to race,
but it was soon evident that a race was in progress. I drove
the Mini to its limit along that narrow twisting road,
praying that nothing was coming the other way. At first
the train had the advantage, then I caught it up and
passed it, then it was the train's turn. On each occasion
there would be a great blast from the engine and the
responding falsetto squeak from the Mini. It was neck
and neck for the next few miles. The driver or fireman
waved from the cab as we rounded each bend. Finally,
we were beaten by half a train-length coming into
Achnasheen. The ensuing whistle blast from the victors
ensured that no one overslept that morning in the soggy
hamlet.

Further on, after Kinlochewe we descended to Glen
Torridon and drew in behind the Ford van at the foot of
Liathach. I let the two dogs out, then, swinging on rucsacks, we set off up the steep, uncompromising face of the
mountain.

The ridge of Liathach is similar to the Aonach Eagach Ridge
in Glencoe: narrow, precipitous and running approximately

east and west. The rock is Torridonian sandstone, some of the oldest rock in the world. It reared above us like a gigantic, rose-coloured plum cake with its serrated ridge sawing a blue sky. Over to our right some men wearing plus-fours, braces and fore-and-aft caps were cutting peats. Their black and white collie barked at Rangi and Tiki. I could just discern, beside the dog, a whisky bottle waiting to fulfil its function – to add vitality to the lot of the Highlander.

Within forty minutes we had reached a point close to the summit ridge. The dogs had been making a wide zigzag search pattern over the rough ground as we ascended. We stopped for a rest and I decided to go down again and double-check a long line of steep sandstone cliffs which curved round the face. It was the sort of place where someone could easily come to grief. As I worked down through a weakness in this rock bluff, Rangi stopped and sniffed, and when I examined a small ledge, the size of a table-mat, I saw an imprint of a cleated rubber sole.

However, there was no other sign, so I made my way back up again, taking a different line. From above there was a shout. It was Catherine.

"Tiki's found him. He's up here."

When I joined her at the top of a scree slope which led to the foot of a steep rocky gully I saw the fallen climber. He was almost invisible, even from a few feet away. His clothing blended perfectly with the brownish-red surroundings.

He was dead all right, and had obviously died a short time after calling, for his watch had stopped at 12.55 p.m. The calls which the two boys had reported hearing from the ridge above were at 12.45 p.m. We sent up a red flare as a signal to John Hinde and the RAF party who had already started up the mountain and sat in the sun on the edge of a small cliff to wait for them. A convoy of tourist cars nudged their way down the glen road, and to my right a golden eagle circled with effortless ease, mocking the inadequacy of man's locomotion.

"Hello, John. Warm day."

"Hi, Hamish, Catherine. So you found the guy?"

"Tiki did. See if you can spot him."

The body was a mere 200 feet away, but none of the RAF boys could locate him until we pointed out where he lay. It was an excellent example of what a good rescue dog can do.

It was a tiring carry to the road and repeated lowers had to be made down sandstone bands. We were all shattered when we reached the vehicles. A few tourists had congregated. The possibility of viewing gore or a corpse always seems to fascinate people. I suppose that was why public executions were such sell-outs in harsher times.

Meanwhile, to the north, more search parties had taken to the hills for George Mack, while Alan Jeffreys and Brian Reid took to the earth. A party of Mack's workmates had also arrived from the Central Electricity Generating Board, Manchester. They had asked Charlie Rhoden for a demanding search. The Inspector, taking them at their word, set them off on George Mack's intended route, but in the opposite direction. When they returned in the evening they were thoroughly exhausted; obviously the mountains of the Scottish Highlands were higher and further apart than those of the Lakes and the Dales.

As I had work to catch up with back home, I couldn't return to Elphin to help the search. But this was continued, tapering off to periodic sorties as months went by. George's mother was much disturbed by the failure to recover her son's body. She consulted a clairvoyant. The medium told her that George was "upside down in a rock crevasse, near the summit, to the north of the mountain". This tract of country is wild and remote with no roads leading into it. However, Donnie Smith and the Police team did in fact search it, but without success. Donnie, always a stickler for map-work, drafted a letter to the medium to seek a map-reference for the exact location of the corpse, but his Chief Constable, Mr Ross, thought better of sending it. Eventually, after ten days and twenty hours of helicopter flying, the main search was abandoned, and to this day George Mack's body has not been recovered.

3

A CASE OF DEDUCTION

In the late 1960s I used to run ice-climbing courses in
Glencoe, teaching winter techniques to both beginners and
established rock climbers. I had a band of top climbers as
instructors and there was always a friendly rivalry as to who
got the star pupils and the new routes. We made many first
ascents in the glen and even further afield in the north-west
of Scotland.

On a course during the winter of 1969 I was lucky enough
to get four good rock-climbing students who were doing their
final year at a London medical school. One was a Chinese
called Dan Chen, a man of bubbling humour with a dedica-
tion to healing and a passion divided between mountaineering and classical music. We did some new routes together
and his influence remains with us in the route names:
'Innuendo' and 'Adagio'. Chris Bonington was climbing in
the glen at the time, attempting a new route on Stob Corie nan
Lochain, and he borrowed Dan and another fledgling doctor
to do Adagio. Adagio, on Stob Coire nam Beith, is close to
the West Face of Aonach Dubh, an imposing piece of mountain architecture, severed by gullies, reinforced by buttresses
and each one labelled for climbers, A through to F. Each
gully and each buttress has been climbed and given a grade
of difficulty and some of the buttresses have several routes on
them. The only easy way up and down is A, or Dinnertime
Buttress, so called because climbers use it as a descent
route, returning for dinner to the Clachaig Inn on the valley
floor.

On 9th September that same year, I was standing outside my cottage when Willie Elliot came up in his Morris

38

Traveller, with its Tudor-cottage woodwork. Willie is always brisk when trouble is brewing.

"Hamish, there's a car at the quarry and it's been there for a couple of days."

"Yes, I saw it, Willie. Trouble?"

"Could be; I had a look in the window. There's quite a bit of climbing gear."

I grunted. "I'll give the law a ring and we'll take a look at it. Wait a mo."

When we opened the car about an hour later we discovered that Willie's through-the-window observations were correct. There was a pile of equipment and it obviously belonged to capable climbers, for it was well used but in first-class order. Also it was apparent that they hadn't taken away all the paraphernalia necessary for a hard route, for there was a good selection of karabiners, slings and chocks still in the vehicle. However, ropes, an essential part of a climber's furniture, were missing, as were the climbing boots, though there were two pairs of PAs, lightweight rock boots, in a rucsack. We then did a fruitless check of the tents in the glen to try and find where they were staying. We assumed that had they been in a hotel or hostel they would have been reported missing by now. Failure to pay one's bill is a great incentive for hoteliers' concern as to their guests' whereabouts the world over.

As the car was in good working order it had obviously not been abandoned and no vehicle of its description had been reported stolen. But as this was before the days of computer checking for car owners we would have to await the then more lengthy process of establishing the owner.

It was obvious that we had to take some action, but where were we to search? Though not apparent to the non-climber, there were clues. Firstly, the missing equipment. We know the normal sort of gear a climber has and it was obvious that their hill boots were missing. Also, there was no guide book. Visiting climbers to the glen would have one. We knew that on the day the car appeared at the quarry at the foot of Aonach Dubh the sky was overcast with a fine drizzle and a strong south-westerly wind. Deducing that climbers of their apparent ability would take such factors into consideration, we narrowed the search field, or rather the number of routes suitable for the then prevailing climatic conditions and the equipment which they had possibly taken with them.

By this time (we are not particularly fast thinkers) it was approaching dusk; nevertheless we set off. I asked various members of the team to take a climb each, of severe standard and lower, all on the West Face of Aonach Dubh, Stob Coire nam Beith area. Any climbs higher up would, we felt, have been uninviting two days before. Ian Clough and Dudley Knowles, who were then both working in Clachaig, were to follow up later and carry the stretcher in case it was required. John Grieve and Alan Fyffe, a climbing instructor, agreed to come up behind Denis Barclay and me to search No 2 Gully, which is to the side of Dinnertime Buttress.

After climbing Dinnertime Buttress with Denis I intended to traverse along a ledge system in the middle of the face, named, as one would expect, Middle Ledge. Willie Elliot was working over to our right with a dog called Corrie, along with Sandy Whillans, our local Police Sergeant and his hound Righ. With them was Walter Elliot and Ralph Blane, a climber who was then working for the National Trust for Scotland.

As we climbed we searched hidden black holes in gullies and in half an hour or so Denis and I came to the start of Middle Ledge, where it cuts round the edge of B Buttress to gain the easier ground beyond. This traverse, awkward at the best of times, was very greasy that night and I came back as I had taken the wrong line. There's a four-storey drop below, so it wasn't the time or place for nocturnal heroics. Once on the right line it was easier, and behind me, Denis talked about a new pair of skis he had just bought. As I stepped across to a foothold some four feet away I thought

I saw something unusual just below. It was. I shouted back
to Denis, "Looks as if we could be on to something, Denis,
I've found a guide book. It hasn't been in residence that
long, otherwise it would be in a much worse state."

There had been a lot of rain at the end of August and had
it been lying out for more than a few days it would have
resembled soggy cigarette paper. I reached down for the
book and, climbing across to the ledge on the other side of
the buttress, I had a look at it, but there were no further
clues. No name in it and it looked fairly new.

"You know, Hamish," Denis said cautiously when he
came across and joined me, "I think maybe I saw a body way
down in the gully bed. But it was too far away to be sure."

"I'll call the others on the radio," I said. "This guide book
could be significant. It definitely fell from above, from a
climb on B Buttress."

Pinnacle Face, one of those climbs, is directly above where
the guide book had been lying. This particular route is greasy
in the wet, and if anyone fell off the climb they would drop
several hundred feet into the gully below. It was a terrible
thought but an unlikely one, I reflected, for, presumably,
they would have been roped, unless, of course, the belay
came off or broke.

We started down, now on the opposite side of the gully
from Dinnertime Buttress, up which was coming a party
comprising Will Thomson, John Hardie, Robin Turner and
Phil Johnson. Walter Elliot's group was heading across
towards us on the other flank. I could hear the dogs snarling
at each other.

Denis and I decided to abseil down into the gully to avoid
a long descent to an easier crossing place, so, putting the
doubled rope round a birch sapling, we lowered ourselves to
a small dripping ledge. We had assumed that the rope would
take us right into the gully bed next abseil. We were wrong.
It was forty feet short when doubled.

Meantime, the Dinnertime Buttress party had cut into the

gully just above us and a shout from Will indicated that he had found the climbers. This is how Will described the scene: "One body was lying crumpled face-up, to the side of the stream, with an arm pointing to the night sky – a macabre sight. The other was propped up against the wall on the other side of the gully. They were still roped."

Phil Johnson, who was next at the scene, asked Will, "How are they?"

Will, not realising that this was Phil's first time on a fatal accident, jokingly told him to give the chap on the other side of the gully the kiss of life. When Phil shone his torch on the body he discovered that the climber was very dead. Poor Phil was then sick. It's not that one is callous and uncaring when dealing with fatalities. The joking, hail-fellow-well-met attitude is a defence mechanism which helps the rescuer to deal with these gruesome situations.

Once it had been established that the two missing climbers were beyond any assistance which our team could offer, those in the gully deigned to listen to our pleas for a rope to get us off the ledge on which we'd marooned ourselves. Various suggestions, mostly unprintable, were made.

It was Robin Turner who first seriously considered our plight and shouted up that if we had a knife he could cut off part of the rope connecting the bodies for our use – they were loath to untie the rope from the bodies. For years I had deplored Denis's habit as a climbing partner of stoking and igniting his pipe in confined spaces like a briny tent, with the accompanying plethora of dead matches. That night I almost forgave him the habit when he suggested that as we had no knife he could lower his lighter on our single rope and Robin could burn the corpses' rope. Will appeared on the scene as the lighter reached the gully and couldn't understand at first what was going on. He thought for a moment that the knots on the climbing rope had tightened so much on the fall that they couldn't be undone. When he found out the circum-stances he exploded, "It's much easier to take the rope off the bodies. I've no bloody qualms about it even if you lot have . . ." In five minutes Denis and I had a spare rope up and abseiled down to the others in the gully.

We sat down and waited for the two stretchers to arrive.

"Don't forget to take that chap's boot down, Robin," Will said.

"Aye, all right," Robin replied, going over to the body. He lifted it up. "Oh," he said in a quiet voice. "There's still a foot in it."

I had found a bar of Cadbury's Fruit and Nut chocolate in the gully bed and had shared it with those not too squeamish to eat. Will, who had returned to a boulder perch just below, saw a nylon tape sling in the beam of his headlamp. He picked it up and I could see him peering at it.

"Hey!" he exclaimed above the din of the water. "There's a name on this. It's ruddy odd, he must be a Chinaman: D. Chen . . ."

I was sitting on my rucsack, for everything else was soaking wet, and now jumped up as if stung by a scorpion. "What, Chen? Dan Chen?" In the beam of a waning torch I studied the features of the body closest to me. Sure enough, it was Dan. I felt stunned. I had regarded Dan as a friend, not as another pupil who had come to Glencoe to learn winter climbing. He was a genius, a genial genius, a man of infinite ability. As if not wanting to believe it I opened the pocket of his anorak. Inside I found a wallet and a driving licence. I studied it with the headlamp and then replaced it slowly. He was only twenty-five. His companion, Peter Groarke, was twenty-one.

All the team were converging on the gully now, for they had heard over the radio that the bodies had been found. John Grieve arrived in a filthy temper. He tends to be black or white in his judgement of worldly and spiritual matters; a born debater and debunker, to whom a spade is a spade. John doesn't like rescue dogs. The fact that one of the dogs got above him in the confines of the gully and showered

rocks down with the accuracy of a medieval siege veteran
didn't do anything to improve John's opinion of four-legged
rescuers. The incident was compounded as the dog's owner
happened to be our local Police Sergeant – another grey if
not black area in John's curriculum.

Last to arrive were Ian Clough and Dudley Knowles, each
carrying a stretcher and sweating.

"What the hell was keeping you bastards?" someone
shouted, though a few minutes before we had commented
on their rapid ascent up Dinnertime Buttress.

"They were probably swilling it down in the pub," someone else rejoined. Ian and Dudley's reply was brief and to
the point.

We heaved the bodies on to the stretchers and decided to
take them down one at a time on the first awkward section,
as we were short of manpower. On easy ground a casualty
can be evacuated with a handful of rescuers, but once back
ropes are used to lower a stretcher down steep terrain, a
good team of skilled rescuers is needed. The steep upper
part of Aonach Dubh that night had to be treated with
respect if another accident was to be avoided. This part of
Dinnertime Buttress is both steep and loose. I asked one of
the volunteers who had come up with the Police party and
didn't have a torch to stay with one body in the gully so that
we could find it more easily when we returned.

After taking the first victim down on to the easier, but still
steep scree, we saw that our 'volunteer' corpse sentry was
with us.

"Hey, what are you doing down here, Jimmy?" I asked.
"You're supposed to be up there with the body." I pointed
up the slope.

"Sorry, but I got a bit frightened on my own in the dark
with that corpse," he muttered apologetically.

Anyhow, we managed to relocate the dead climber and
whilst we were taking him down we almost lost a member of
the Argyll County Police. This constable, no doubt more at

home on some tranquil beat or in a patrol car than on the pitch-black face of Aonach Dubh, slipped on ball-bearing scree. His headlamp arched like a mono-coloured rainbow as he gyrated. He would have gone over a cliff had it not been for the spontaneous reactions of Ian Clough, who grabbed him by his anorak and probably saved his life. Two separate stretcher parties now picked their way down the hillside above the Elliots' house. To the west the lights of Glencoe village twinkled at the stars and we could see the headlights of the ambulance and the police Land-Rover in front of the cottage. Even here, literally a stone's throw from the comfort of a warm fire, the mountain still had to have the last say. Large boulders dislodged by the top stretcher party thundered down the slope. One of the problems of trying to dodge falling rocks at night is that you can't see them. I suppose it's something like facing a firing squad blindfolded, wondering where the first thudding impact is going to come. It is a frightening experience. By a miracle no one was hit, but the stretcher was badly damaged.

We never did find out what caused the accident which killed Dan and Peter, but it seems likely that Dan fell and pulled Peter off too, for Peter's belay loop was still attached to his harness. Possibly the rock bollard that Peter used broke off or his sling pulled off it when Dan's weight came on him.

We were depressed that we hadn't found the two men alive; taking bodies down is always a sombre and negative task. But we did learn something: that our line of reasoning for locating the climbers had been correct and, who knows, perhaps next time round similar deduction may save someone's life. To me, personally, it was a tragic finale for Peter and Dan.

4

BIG TOP AND THE HIGH WIRE ACT

17th August 1971 was a Saturday. I was standing outside my workshop nattering to Douglas Lang and Sidney Littleford from Dundee. It had been a peaceful day . . .

The telephone rang. "Oh, no," I said to them. "It is a Saturday after all . . ." My fears were confirmed when I picked up the receiver. It was Willie Elliot. I knew the formula by the tone of his voice.

"There's been an accident on Aonach Dubh, Hamish, on Big Top. The climber is supposed to be hanging by his legs near the top of the climb."

This was a new slant. We have had climbers hanging from their waists and even from their necks, where they had been as effectively executed as by a hangman, but never had one hanging from his legs. My mind boggled at the possibilities.

"This could be serious, Willie," I said, without realising how ridiculous my observation was. "Call the lads out. I'll be down in a brace of shakes. OK, you two," I told my companions. "Come and see how the other half lives in Glencoe and how we get our exercise." I told them briefly what had happened and they dashed off to their doss, the Rannoch Club hut, to get their gear while I grabbed a selection of equipment I thought would be necessary for the operation, as I knew it could be a technical rescue. At that time, Big Top was one of the most serious rock climbs in Scotland. It takes an intimidating line up the sheer flank of E Buttress, a great tombstone-shaped rock rising high above the Elliots' tiny cottage. We had done a live TV outside broadcast from it a short time before and had in fact left a helipad in place which we had cut from the high-angled flank of F Buttress opposite, just across No 4 Gully from Big Top. Some day, we had thought, it might serve us in a rescue operation. The chance to test it had come sooner rather than later.

Just a few years before, such a rescue would have been a serious problem, but we had perfected a technique using a cableway system of evacuating casualties from faces. Indeed, we now found that the steeper the location, the easier it was to get someone off smoothly. Nevertheless, I didn't underestimate the impending problem, especially if, as reported, the climber was hanging upside down. If this were the case, we would be collecting another corpse. In 1971 climbing harnesses weren't common, and a climber hanging free after a fall with a rope round his waist would be dead in minutes. But if the casualty were unconscious, there was a different set of problems for his second. Even if the second is able to secure the victim, it isn't always the best thing to rush off for help, leaving the unconscious person in an exposed place – or indeed even on easy ground. If they regain consciousness they are usually confused and sometimes attempt to move. This situation had occurred several times over the years in the glen. Once, when a climber fell in the Chasm of Buachaille Etive Mor, his companion managed to pendulum him on to a ledge, but didn't have enough spare rope to secure him there. He ran down for help with his friend still unconscious from head injuries. The injured man must have revived during this time, for when we got to him he had swung back across the face on the rope and was dead.

Douglas and Sidney returned, we jumped into the car and drove down the glen to the Elliots' house. At that time I was living at my cottage at the Meeting of Three Waters, opposite the Lost Valley, so it wasn't far to travel.

"Aye," Willie greeted us as we skidded to a halt on the loose gravel.

"Any more news, Willie?" I asked, getting out of the van.

"Aye, the chap isn't hanging as first reported," Willie returned. "He's managed to get on to a ledge on the last pitch. I haven't seen anybody else up there, but I've spied him with my glass." The aforementioned item, his telescope, was in fact tucked, Nelson fashion, under his arm. The telescope is a vital appendage to all Highland stalkers and keepers who ensure, with its dexterous use, that nothing is private, even in the remotest corrie.

Apparently the climber had 'peeled' when a loose block came away in his hands and had fallen in a long pendulum and, according to the man who had reported it, was in fact upside down at one stage.

As part of my work is designing rescue equipment, I often take the opportunity of real live rescues to test various items. In this way the gear is used with the greatest possible stress, which is difficult to achieve in a test. I'm sure patients have never regretted being guinea pigs, for so far over almost twenty-five years we have managed to get them down without anyone dying during an evacuation. This time I had hatched up a new type of stretcher to take on an Everest expedition the following year. For years I had resisted designing a stretcher which split in two, maintaining that there was just a chance that one half wouldn't reach the casualty should the team get split up. However, John Grieve, one of our active team members, had prevailed upon me and the result was the shiny complexity of Hiduminium tubes which I now took out of the van.

"We'll have to get all this stuff up, Willie." I piled out ropes and other ironmongery on the grass beside the stretcher.

"Doris did a full call-out; there will be a fair squad," Willie reported.

There was a fair squad as Willie had predicted, and soon the pastoral scene of the field beside the loch with its cows and sheep was augmented with parked cars. Even with the fifteen or so team members that had arrived, we still had further gear to carry. Just then a beat-up van shuddered to a halt and we recognised some of the 'Glencoe Steam Team', as they were called, hard climbers, who, like the 'Bendy-Bendy Boys' (who lived under a very low bridge near my cottage), were often out with us on rescues.

"Di ye want a hand?" One of them spoke with a strong Glaswegian accent.

"Help yourself," I said, pointing to half the stretcher and a rope. "They have to be delivered posthaste to the top of E Buttress."

"Aye, awricht." They tumbled out of their Mini van.

We decided to take a long route up into the edge of the Bidean Corrie, then back along a ledge system to F Buttress. This is the next 'tombstone' to the right of E Buttress when viewed from the tarmac of the A82. It was a fine evening, the sort that every good Highland midge rejoices in, as it ensures that she will be eating out of doors with so many humans about. We didn't have to use headlamps and when I felt the midges having supper I recollected that I hadn't had a meal since early morning.

"Any grub with you?" I asked Willie Elliot who was just in front.

"Not a sausage. I haven't had my tea yet."

"How about you, Walter?" I quizzed his brother.

"Oh, I had my tea, Hamish." There was a tinge of contentment in his voice like the purring of a well-fed cat.

"Some bastards are psychic about these things," some wag cut in. "Walter has a hot line to the Almighty."

"No such thing," Walter replied, flicking some ash off his cigarette. "I simply had an early tea."

It's always easy to be smart after the event. I should, as tolerated leader of the team, have left someone to point out the way, where we cut horizontally across the huge West Face of Aonach Dubh, for there is only one line of weakness from this direction, the Upper Ledge. I assumed, wrongly, that all the team and the 'Glencoe Steam Team' knew this

route. The result was that two of the 'Steam Team' volunteers went astray and it wasn't until five hours later that we
realised they were missing, with half the stretcher!

The live TV broadcast we had recently made on Big Top
meant we were very well acquainted with the details of this
superb rock climb and now once more we approached the
helipad on F Buttress opposite, which we had excavated for
ferrying in our equipment. I call it a helipad; actually it was
a toehold for the helicopter – there was room for part of one
skid with a nick cut out of the rock above to accommodate
the helicopter rotor. It wasn't the sort of place where you
would make a fortune running joy rides.

When we reached the helipad we put both searchlights on.
Powerful quartz halogen beams sliced the night. In seconds
they homed in on a crouching figure hanging like a spider
belayed on its gossamer, dozing and waiting for its next
customer. It didn't doze for long.

"For Christ's sake, turn those bloody things off or I'll have
to put on my sunglasses!"

"Well!" Jimmy Brown, a constable in the Argyll Police
team, boomed. "At least we won't be taking back a corpse."

"Dinna be too sure," someone else rejoined. "It's amazing whet we can do when we try."

"Hello," I called. "Are you all right?"

"Is that you, Hamish?" came a reply from the bundle of
suspended animation. "It's Jimmy McDowell."

"Yes, Jim. I've all the lads here. What are your injuries?"

"Hell, I'm sorry, lads," he returned apologetically. "But I
seem to have hurt my ankle. I certainly can't put any weight
on it."

"I wouldn't worry about that," John Grieve called back.
"I did mine in going through a roof helping MacInnes
here get some scrapwood. It sounds better doing it on Big
Top."

Jim had been on an expedition to the Polish Tatra with
one of my climbing instructors, Jim McArtney, who had

been killed in an accident on Ben Nevis. In fact, the last time I had met Jim McDowell prior to this nocturnal exercise was when I had picked him up in Elgin to attend Jim's funeral.

Most of the team had arrived by now and there was the usual cracking of jokes. Most of them knew Jim, who was a leading climber, and he became the subject of their repartee. I shouted to him again. "If we get a set of jumars and a couple of ropes down to you, Jim, do you think that you could climb on your own?" A jumar clamp holds only in one direction on a rope and acts like a moving handhold. There was a pause.

"I could try, but I think it might be easier to go down."

"I doubt if we can do that, Jim, we haven't enough rope; it's a hell of a way down into the gully from where you're hanging. Anyhow, just hold on, we're coming over."

"He hasn't much bloody option but to hold on, has he?" Will Thomson observed.

We had a meeting of the team shareholders to debate the position and eventually agreed that a couple of us should abseil down to Jim with a spare set of jumars and try to get him to the top of the buttress, for he was reasonably close to the top of the climb.

Will Thomson, his brother Dave, John Hardie, Walter Elliot, John Grieve and Robin Turner came over with me to the top of the buttress, while the others waited in this airy auditorium, watched us and exhausted their vast repertoire of dirty jokes. Having taken Police courses for many years I've found that they have a computer-like memory for dirty jokes. Peals of laughter echoed up the face of Aonach Dubh. From where we were at the top of E Buttress it sounded as if the Lord of the Mountain had a late licence, and I heard the taunting broad Glaswegian voice of the 'Weed' ring out – he was a member of the 'Steam Team'.

"Hey, Jimmy, di ye ken that young Alec is awa wi' yer wuman?"

Every so often a 'grounded' team member would remind

the victim of his responsibilities to the community and to them in particular . . . "Ye'll be owing us some beer for this nicht, McDowell." The casualty's replies were equally pointed and left little to the imagination.

Alasdair MacDonald, a local shepherd, had a small fire going on the helipad and Sandy Whillans, our local Police Sergeant, and Willie Elliot decided to make use of the casualty bag, for the night was getting an edge to it. Willie took a walkie-talkie in beside him "to keep it warm", he said. Jimmy Brown, the large Gaelic-speaking policeman from Dalmally, shone the searchlight on this ungainly casualty bag bundle on the ledge and boomed: "Hey, lads, look at this. Our Sergeant is feeling amorous – he's gone to bed wi' Willie Elliot!" Later, when Jimmy Brown grew fed up with the repetitive nature of Glaswegian invective where that much abused four-letter word connected with the conception of life peppers every sentence, he admonished them, saying, "You lads should learn the Gaelic, it's much more expressive." As we were belaying the 200-foot rope which we had taken over with us for the abseil, we could hear that the discourse had now changed to the colour problem on Clydeside and how Pakistanis made good Gaelic-speaking crofters.

Robin Turner, who had taken over one of the searchlights, leaned over the face and could just pick out Jim's foot sticking out from the ledge some seventy feet below.

"We'll be down in a few minutes, Jim," I called. "Just sorting out the gear."

In about half an hour, for the Highland minute is very elastic, we had peg belays in place for the rope. I put on my rucsack and abseiled down. Will had me belayed on a safety rope. I heard Cecil MacFarlane's voice issuing from the void below. "Just as well it's dark, lads, I'd be scared silly up here in daylight."

Across on the helipad Douglas Lang switched on the other searchlight. As I went down over the edge I shouted to John

Grieve who was ready to abseil behind me. "Can you take the radio with you, John? It'll save our lungs."

"Right."

It felt eerie spiralling down through the floodlit night. It was like descending into a pool of light with limitless darkness beyond. I could see Jim below my heels. He was tied to a piton beside the flake which was the belay for that pitch. It wasn't really a ledge he was on, more a sloping shelf – sloping the wrong way – a built-in ejection seat, the sort of place where one is always being nudged by gravity to take a one-way ticket.

I was worried that when I came level with him I would be too far out from the face to swing into his stance, but as I pendulumed, he grabbed my rope and pulled me to him.

"Thanks." Before I did anything else I put a piton in. "That's a bit better. How's your belay?"

"Not very good." I shone my headlamp on his shaky-looking piton and hastened to agree. "But I'm also tied to a chock on the other side of you," he added.

"I've got a spare pair of jumars with me; do you think you can manage up with a tight top rope?"

"Well," he said. "I thought perhaps I could, until I saw you coming down, away from the face. I have my doubts; I seem to be weaker than I thought."

"You must be." Shock alone can play havoc with one's physical condition. "Well, the other thing I can suggest," I ventured, "is that we take you across the gully on a 500-foot cableway, over to the helipad, where the searchlights are. It will certainly be the quickest and easiest way, much better than attempting to go down."

I don't think Jim replied to this; possibly he wasn't too enthusiastic about the idea! I shouted across to those on the helipad.

"Hey, how much rope do you have?"

"The 500-foot non-stretch rescue rope," came the reply from someone, "and it's on its way to the top of E Buttress."

"There should be at least one other 200-foot rope," I yelled back. "Where the hell has it gone to?"

There was a pause and I could see headlamps probing the night on F Buttress.

"No other rope here," came the reply. "It must have been left down below."

I was sure that it hadn't for I had checked all the gear before we left the Elliots' field.

"Have you got a fag, Hamish?" Jim asked.

"Don't smoke, Jim, but I'll shout to John Grieve to bring one down. Walter Elliot may have some." I conveyed this request to John.

"I'll see what I can do," came the reply. "Filthy habit!"

A scraping noise above heralded the descent of John Grieve. My headlamp lit the pebbles jammed between the rubber cleating of his Vibram-soled boots. My thoughts, however, were on the immediate problem of rigging the cableway. The best solution was to anchor one end of the 500-foot rope at the top of the climb, have the other end passed down to us, then we'd lower it into the gully. The helipad crew could retrieve this end, take it across to F Buttress and tension it, once Jim was attached. He would then be swung away from the face towards F Buttress and Will Thomson's gang above would then lower Jim on the safety line down the cableway. That is if we had enough rope!

As John swung in beside us I looked up once more.

"Hey, look, John!" I pointed up to the face high above the helipad, realising as I did so that he couldn't see my arm.

"The lights?"

"Yes, they must be some of our party gone astray. I bet they had too much to drink at the Clachaig."

But we had too much to get on with at hand to be over-concerned about the lost and strayed.

"Here's your fag, Jim, and a box of matches."

"Thanks, John."

"John, how about getting those above on the radio to send down a rucsack with some rocks in it?" I suggested. "That'll ensure that we lower the end of the 500-foot rope directly into the gully; otherwise it might snag."

"Good idea."

This operation worked well. The F Buttress searchlight followed the descent of the rucsack and, after some climbing by those below, it was retrieved together with the end of the 500-foot rope. With the ropes that John and I had used to come down, plus the other on top, we thought we had just sufficient to lower Jim. It was going to be close.

While those above and below were working on their allotted tasks, I splinted Jim's ankle. He was already wearing a climbing harness, so we only had to add a chest loop to prevent him hanging back when attached to the suspension rope. We clipped a small pulley to both the body and chest harness and attached them to the cableway. Next, John secured the end of the safety rope to Jim's harness. The rest of this rope had been pulled to the top by Will Thomson's party. It was all stations go . . .

"OK, Will. Take in his safety rope tightly."

"That's it," came the reply. By the light of our lamps we saw tension come on this rope and Jim was partially lifted off the ledge. We had released him from his belay and were now holding him with a long sling which acted as a painter. Once we got those below to tension the cableway he was going to swing far out from the face as the rope at present took a dog-leg back across the gully towards the helipad. The operation had taken a great deal of time and I suddenly realised that it would soon be dawn. I asked John Hardie and the boys on top if they were ready.

"OK, Hamish," Will's voice came over the walkie-talkie.

"OK below, Hamish," said Dudley Knowles. "Just let us know when you want the 500-foot rope tensioned."

"I'll do that, Dud."

John and I started to ease Jim round a nose of rock. We

had virtually nothing to stand on at this point and had little
help from the searchlights as they tended to dazzle us during
the operation. Now we had him hanging free. Jim started to
swing.

"Are you OK?" I shouted.

"Yes, seems to be fine," he said. "There's a bit of turbulence."

"Right, Dud," I called over the walkie-talkie, though he
probably heard me shouting in any case. "More tension."

The suspension rope whipped into life as four hefty climbers below exerted their full weight on it. Jim shot out into
space away from the rock and hung there as if he was up for
auction, highlighted by the searchlights. It was an exciting
few moments as he slowly stopped swinging and hung
poised. The bottom end of the 500-foot suspension rope
went through a karabiner clip attached to pitons. Denis
Barclay, who was closest to them, was alarmed to see one of
the pegs pull out of a crack in slow motion; thankfully the
other held.

I barked into the radio mike, "You can lower now, Will,
fast as you like."

The lowering rope ran through John Hardie's hands so
rapidly that he had to slow it down to prevent being burned,
despite his gloves. From our ledge we watched Jim get
smaller as he descended. I asked Dud to slacken the suspension rope a bit. When this was done, Jim descended at a
steeper angle and, within a few minutes, was actually lower
than Dud's anchor party, for the gully fell abruptly from the
lower position. Other members of the team reached up
and grasped Jim as he hung above them; they asked John
Hardie, over the radio, to release the safety rope. When this
was done, Jim was put down on a sloping ledge in the gully
and his safety rope taken off.

After a few minutes, with the aid of the suspension rope
which ran up the bed of the gully to Dud's party, Jim
half-pulled, half-crawled to this higher position with very

little help. I think that he was overjoyed at last to be doing something towards his own salvation.

Meantime, John and I were faced with the problem of getting off the climb. We had to go up for it was too dangerous to double rope off. Though we would have liked to go down on the cableway, the 500-foot rope was away from our position now and it could have taken too long to get it across to us again. There was nothing for it but to go back up a rope to the top of the wall.

"Hey, Will," I spoke into the radio. "Chuck down a couple of ropes when you retrieve them. We want to get back home for our porridge."

"Dinna be impatient, laddie," Will's voice echoed from above. "It'll be doon in a meenute."

It was John Hardie who shouted down next.

"There's a couple of ropes coming down. Watch your heads."

The words were scarcely uttered when two rope ends whistled past our ears. We grabbed them when they swung in on their initial momentum and in about a minute I was tied on to one and had fixed my jumar clamps on to the other. Over the radio John Grieve told Will which rope was which and I soon felt a reassuring tug on the safety rope.

I started to ascend, first sliding one clamp up, standing in the loop attached to it, then moving up the other jumar. I was soon free of the face and as both ropes were of hawser-laid construction – that is three main twisted strands rather than the modern climbing rope with braided sheath – they started to twist despite the fact that John was holding them apart below. It was only when I got up under the overhang in that grey light that I managed to 'unwind'. I did this by lying back horizontally so that I got the tips of my toes on the bulge and did a contra-rotating act. By the time I got up I was thinking, What a bloody circus – I'm cast as Coco the Clown! As I looked down on the twisted ropes they reminded me of tightly wound propeller elastic in a kid's

model plane. John didn't fare any better than me, actually a
lot worse.

When we reached the helipad back on F Buttress, albeit a
bit dizzy, the others were having an impromptu ceilidh, and
our casualty was leaning back on a rucsack as if waiting for
MacBrayne's bus to Glasgow.

"What was keeping you lazy buggers?" someone asked.

Robin Turner spoke. "Hamish, I have to inform you, as
honorary designer of MacInnes stretchers, that only half of
the latest model is here . . ."

Someone suggested that we lop the patient in two like
Procrustes did and come back to collect the other half.

I turned to John Grieve. "John, those lights which we saw
higher up the face, they must have belonged to some of the
'Steam Team'."

"Aye," Willie Elliot cut in. "Three of the 'Steam Team'
headed directly up the face instead of coming along the
Upper Ledge."

Luckily the part of the stretcher we had was the runner
section and by threading the tubes through sleeves of two
anoraks, to act as a stretcher bed, a tolerable litter was
manufactured. A rather incongruous entourage made its
way back Upper Ledge. Someone was singing 'The Ball of
Kerriemuir' and the patient was told not to complain or he'd
be dumped.

As we were slanting down into the entrance of the Bidean
Corrie, Denis shouted, "Hey, look, there are some people
higher up." Sure enough, three figures could be seen on the
steep face above. They still had their now dim headlamps
on; these were just discernible in the morning light. Shouting, we managed to attract their attention and told them how
to get down to us. We met up with them about half an hour
later. They were the missing 'Steam Team' members. We
reassembled the stretcher and Jim was installed on a slightly
more gracious and comfortable means of transport, held safe
in a 'cage' of six longitudinal tubes, reminiscent of the bars

that used to be put over graves to deter body snatchers. Indeed, in that eerie dawn light we could easily have passed for a band of resurrectionists, only our 'snatch' still had a lot of life in him.

Now it was only a matter of sweating, swearing and slithering down the steep path to the Elliots' cottage, where an ambulance was waiting. Two pure white swans floated motionless on Loch Achtriochtan at the doorstep of the cottage. We climbed into our cars to return home for breakfast and, for quite a few of us, a day's work.

Denis Barclay later described this rescue in a nutshell, "There were some good laughs that night."

5

OSSIAN'S CAVE

One fact which has been brought home to me in compiling this book is that, after the event, team members recall quite different aspects of the same rescue. Obviously they are most conscious of what they actually witness and at night in a winter blizzard it can be very little. Often it's only the area swept by their headlamp, supplemented by cryptic messages over the walkie-talkie.

The Ossian's Cave affair has special memories for Ronnie Rodger. It was his first rescue and coincidentally it was his great-great-grandfather, Nicol Marquis, who had been the first man to enter the cave high on the north side of Aonach Dubh in 1868. No one believed that he had done it until the respected pioneer climber, Professor Norman Collie, substantiated Nicol's claim by identifying the handkerchief the agile shepherd of Achtriochtan had left tied to a sapling at the entrance. The somewhat dismissive professor described the shepherd as a gruff and inarticulate man. The truth was that Nicol Marquis could hardly speak English, Gaelic being his native tongue.

The cave is a lofty place, visible from the A82 by the side of Loch Achtriochtan, and it would be condemned as a dwelling for even someone as robust as Ossian. If the legendary Gaelic bard did write an ode there, his metres would have suffered from both rising and falling damp, while its 150-foot entrance ensures that it welcomes in even the least suspicion of northerly winds. The floor is steeply angled and the cave is quite shallow. In fact, it isn't a cave at all, but the hole left by a basalt dyke which has fallen away. It is now approached by a steep vegetated ramp which requires some rudimentary climbing skills and considerable faith in tree roots and flora to complete the ascent safely. Needless to say, we don't recommend it for a post-prandial stroll.

9th June 1972 was one of those balmy spring days when the good Lord seems reluctant to turn off the lights. Just as well, for we had a busy time on the steep northern slopes of Aonach Dubh. A group of thirty-five from the Hermitage Academy in Helensburgh were staying in Hugh McColl's bunkhouse, next to the Youth Hostel.

Twelve boys and girls set off with a master, who had done some climbing, to ascend to the cave. There was also a gym teacher in attendance who had no mountaineering experience. They set off at 6.00 p.m. which must be one of the latest starts on record for such a group in our area.

Willie and Walter Elliot, who were coming down the main road in their Morris Traveller, saw a minibus drawing in at a lay-by opposite Aonach Dubh at about 7.45 p.m. The two brothers stopped in the same lay-by to check some sheep on the face of the Aonach Eagach Ridge with their telescopes. The driver of the minibus came over and spoke to them.

"Have you seen a school party of fourteen coming down from Ossian's Cave?" he asked.

"No," Willie replied. "When did they leave?"

"Six o'clock."

"Well, if they left at six," Willie responded, "they won't be down for a while yet and it'll be in the dark!"

"I was told they would be down by eight o'clock and I was to meet them here."

Willie and Walter knew that there was no way a large party could go up to the cave and come down in two hours. They felt worried. Through their telescopes they could see a group at the bottom of Ossian's Ladder leading up the steep section to the cave, but it was impossible to know what was going on. There seemed to be very little action and they decided to return later and have a further 'spy'.

The first I knew of an accident was when a hill walker raised the alarm at the Elliots' cottage. He had been on the lower slopes of the face when some kids shouted down to him. They needed help. The master had fallen. He had been pulled off when belaying one of the girls on Ossian's Ladder. They thought he was still alive and two of their friends were giving him first-aid.

We learnt later that the gym teacher, Miss Sheila McBeth, who lacked the climbing ability to get to her colleague herself, had told some of the children to go down for help, but "to take care and not to hurry". Four of them had descended the steep and rather dangerous route and one of them, thirteen-year-old Jean Winning, who had been told to go only to the end of the dog-leg traverse, got separated from the others, fell a hundred feet on to steep scree and broke her leg. Her cries for help were heard by the other three who traversed over and put a jacket over her.

In 1972 helicopter rescue in Scotland hadn't really got into its swing. The Whirlwinds, though good for their time, were unreliable, and we could never be sure if one would materialise, even in good weather. On this occasion it didn't. Anyhow, by 9 p.m., long shadows were leaving the summits as we crossed the river at Achtriochtan, where 104 years before a soft-spoken Highland shepherd had also set off for Ossian's Cave.

I was with Ian Clough, Ronnie Rodger, Walter Elliot and Kenny Spence. A couple of days before, Kenny had mentioned to John Grieve that if we needed a hand on a call-out, to fetch him from the Dray, the local hideout of the Squirrel Climbing Club from Edinburgh. Kenny is a lithe climber of immeasurable talent with whom I have shared many stances. When he was working with me on the winter climbing courses he made up one of a trio with Alan Fyffe and myself where, in true busman's holiday tradition, we did new snow and ice routes at the weekends with the intervening five days teaching step cutting and cramponing to long-suffering pupils. Kenny has a laconic sense of humour and, despite the gravity of the present situation, he was in good spirits, mainly because the young constable who had been sent to recruit his talents encountered a great deal of trouble in finding the Dray and had squelched into one of the many bogs that plague the way. Only a short time before, Kenny had caused considerable consternation to Willie Elliot who had spotted Kenny's bicycle in the middle of the rising River Coe just after closing time at the Clachaig Inn. I had been able to enlighten him when he 'phoned and I told him that I had not lost one of my instructors for Kenny was sitting before me. The chain, he said, had kept coming off his bike, so he just got fed up and threw the machine into the river.

I had been told of the call-out by Mrs Elliot, but I also had a 'phone call from Dan Stewart, an old friend and a very able climber of vast experience, formerly the Flight Lieutenant in charge of the RAF Kinloss mountain rescue team. Dan was worried as he had just heard that his daughter was in the group which had gone up to the cave, and he knew it was a grotty place, unsuited for a kid's after-dinner excursion. I told him of the call-out and that I'd be in touch as soon as I could come up with some news.

We moved fast up the long ramp which leads to the dog-leg traverse to the bottom of Ossian's Ladder, spurred by the urgency that someone was possibly dying. As I glanced behind I could see other team members crossing the river: Dudley Knowles, the philosophy student working at Clachaig, and Huan Findlay, a staunch, strong farmer who lived at Achtriochtan farm directly below us on the road side of the river.

There were calls above, just to our left, off the normal ascent route. It was the injured girl with her companions. When we got to her we quickly assessed her injuries and as her condition wasn't serious I told them to stay where they were and some of the team would take care of her when they came up. I radioed base and told the young Police constable on duty where she was lying. He would pass the word on for her to be taken down on one of the stretchers.

The day before had been wet, very wet, the sort of rain that must have given inspiration to Noah for his Ark. Now (9th June) it was an enchanted twilight, as if yesterday's naughty-boy weather had never existed. But I knew that all wasn't well just above. I had that gut feeling which I sometimes get when it's a lost cause, when we're too late.

The scenery on the North Face of Aonach Dubh is spectacular. It comprises a series of steeply angled ledges like steps, connected by vertical walls. It's not the place to fall off and it's not a pleasant place to conduct an evacuation. Some time before, just to our right, we had found the almost dismembered body of a hill walker who had crashed over one or possibly two of these connecting faces. His fate and that of other victims of this face are well summed up in the words of Robert Burns's 'Tam O' Shanter':

> Wi' mair o' horrible and awfu',
> Which even to name wad be unlawfu'.

"Looks as if this is a kind of Pied Piper's outing," I said to Ian breathlessly. Ahead of us was a gaggle of schoolkids, some now feeling the chill of a clear evening.

"Where's the chap who fell?" Ian asked a tall, gangly lad.

"Along the ledge a bit and below the start of the way up to the cave."

When we got there we found that the teacher had landed out from the start of Ossian's Ladder and was lying precariously on steep scree. He must have fallen at least 180 feet! There were a boy and girl beside him, both splattered with blood.

"Thank goodness," the girl exclaimed when she saw us. She sat down obviously exhausted. They had both been giving him mouth-to-mouth and cardiac massage for over an hour. These two had shown incredible calmness and single-ness of purpose in administering first-aid to their teacher, for they were both only in their early teens; often we find adults at a loss in such a situation.

We immediately set to work to try to resuscitate him. I got the oxygen unit out of my pack for I thought there was the faintest glimmer of a pulse. Despite all our efforts, he died. It's possible that he passed away minutes after our arrival.

In the meantime, a steady stream of rescuers was toiling up the hillside. I had asked Eric Moss some time before to carry up our portable searchlight from the truck as well as a smaller one. Eric, testing their respective weights, decided, I can't do the dirty and carry the light one, and shouldered the twenty-five-pound battery pack. He gave the light one to Jim Mackay, a volunteer who was at that time working for the National Trust for Scotland.

I contacted Eric on the radio, telling him to wait by the edge of the gully at the start of the traverse to the cave. Due to the previous heavy rain, this section was now particularly nasty and I had remarked earlier to Ian that it was surprising that more of the kids hadn't come to grief there. Certainly now, in the dark, it was going to present a problem in evacuating the body. The remainder of the schoolkids still had to be taken down so I asked a couple of team members to take care of them in order to leave the rest of us free to manhandle the stretcher.

Ian Clough had gone back along to the gully and was hammering in pegs for anchors when we arrived. We had decided to take the stretcher across it by means of a short cableway. This Tyrolean traverse operation was conducted in the glare of two searchlights from across the gully.

Rory MacDonald, who was then owner of the Clachaig Inn, was on our side of the gully resplendent in kilt; with him was John Grey. On the other side were Willie Elliot, Will

Thomson, Eric Moss and Huan Findlay. Huan is a good man to have around when a pull is required!

Somehow, in the confusion, and there was a lot of water coming down to add to the difficulties, we almost had another accident. I shouted for the rope to be tightened from the other side when the stretcher was poised on the edge of the drop, but this message was misinterpreted and the rope went slack. As the stretcher was only balanced on its rocky perch by the rope, it slewed down as soon as the rope went slack and almost swept those of us on the downhill side of it off the rock like so many skittles. However, our dead passenger came to no harm and we quickly regained our equilibrium by grabbing the rope, which immediately went taut as those across the gully realised the problem, so all was well. As usual, instead of blaming someone for the incident, everyone roared with laughter, especially one poor unfortunate who had swung into the water.

After the Tyrolean traverse, we were on home ground with only a few stunted cliffs to avoid or descend. Walter, who knows the face as only one who has tended sheep on it for twenty-five years can, took us on a long traversing descent to the east. I, for one, was thankful that we had a good shepherd to guide us.

6

CORRIE OF THE SPOILS

Coire Gabhail is more generally known these days as the 'Lost Valley' than by its Gaelic name which means 'Corrie of the Spoils'. According to tradition, it was used in freer times as a 'larder' by the MacDonalds of Glencoe to stash away stolen or reived cattle. The MacDonalds, like many of the indigenous tribes of the Highlands, preferred stealing to the rearing of cattle; at least they found the former easier and more lucrative. Reiving also had a spice of adventure which appealed to their basic instincts.

The Lost Valley enters this story via the summit of Buachaille Etive Mor, that stark but stately guardian of the eastern approach to the glen. I had just finished a climb on its flanks one scorching August day in 1973. The rock was kiln dry, as was my throat, and a low heat-haze extended across the Moor of Rannoch to distant Shiehalion.

As I neared the summit I disturbed a blue hare. At the cairn there was old orange peel and a discarded bottle, the label of which proclaimed that it once contained 'Sheep Dip', the whisky, not the sheep de-bugger. There were also two young men in their twenties, one in light-coloured trousers and a tartan shirt, the other sporting blue jeans and a pullover.

"Hi there." It was the light-trousered one who spoke.

"It's a fine day," I returned.

It transpired that they had come up the mountain the easy way, by Coire na Tulaich opposite Altnafeadh, a treadmill of red scree in summer, a snow receptacle in winter, and they planned to traverse the main peaks of the Buachaille, which are linked by a freeway-like ridge running south towards Loch Etive.

"It's an easy walk," I told them. "It'll take you about an hour."

I bade them farewell and took myself down the top of Coire na Tulaich, up which they had slogged, but which for me was more like going down an escalator.

It is a basic law of mountain rescue that call-outs come at the most inconvenient time – when you are in bed, during a storm or blizzard, just when you are going out to a restaurant or perhaps when you are in a bath. We can recollect other times too when a wall is half-painted or a pile of newly mixed cement is left as a fast-setting monument to the particular crisis.

At 5.00 p.m. that evening it wasn't so bad. I had just committed a steak to the frying pan for an early meal. The Police had 'phoned to say they had a 999 call from a party who had heard shouts for help in the Lost Valley. Apparently this group had traversed the summit of Bidean and made their exit from the tops via the Lost Valley. It was on the valley floor that they heard the calls and though they scanned the East Face of Gearr Aonach, where they thought the cries came from, they saw nothing.

I called Willie Elliot and told him about it. "It's most likely a false alarm, Willie, but I'd better go up and have a look around. It's not worth calling out the team."

"Aye, its probably one of my sheep," Willie replied in his down-to-earth fashion. "Will I stand by with a radio at base?"

"Yes, you do that, I'll take a walkie-talkie with me."

In those days we had only five radios, four of which were working. Placing the lump of rare steak in a plastic bag I stuffed it into my anorak pocket and pulled on my boots again. At least, I thought, I may as well make a picnic out of it.

I met Willie in his estate car at a lay-by on the main road and wound down my window. "Where will you be, Willie?"

"I'll stay on the road just below the gorge, Hamish. It should be good reception from there."

"Fine. I just saw Jim MacKay on the way up, he'll come later."

It was a fine evening. At least the midges thought so, for they were ravenous. Climbing up to the Lost Valley, I met several late walkers blistering off the hill from the sun and sore feet, but none of them had heard any calls.

I think the Lost Valley gets its alias from the fact that its floor cannot be seen from the A82. Indeed it is hidden until one emerges from the cyclopean rock debris which chokes the entrance. Then the valley unfolds, an open area about the size of a playing field, quite out of keeping in this up-and-down country. On either side the faces of Beinn Fhada and Gearr Aonach rise over 900 feet to their respective crests, and ahead, more leisurely, the flats revert to a V, later to feed into the U of a gorge.

On the left, the Beinn Fhada Ridge curves round the head of the valley and dips to a pass, then rises slowly, as if feeling the altitude, to the summit of Bidean nam Bian. On the right of the valley, the Gearr Aonach Ridge scales the summit of Stob Coire nan Lochain and one of this peak's ridges then joins hands with Bidean across another pass.

At the other end of the flat area I saw two figures outside a small orange tent, both wearing balaclavas. It was a warm evening, but I realised that the Ku-Klux-Klan gear was a midge prophylactic. Here in the still of the corrie the midges were homing in on any human stupid enough to be abroad.

As I approached, I caught the whiff of an instant curry emanating from a dixie atop a primus.

"Hello there," I greeted. "Have you heard any calls for help?"

"No," one of the crouching figures replied, "but we're just back from the Bealach Dearg." This was the pass at the head of the valley, the Red Pass. He pronounced this

Bee-lak Dee-arg. The other man, the stirrer, looked up from his creation. "Didn't we see you on the summit of the Buck-ale today?"

I didn't attempt to correct his pronunciation of this almost sacred mountain.

"Yes, of course. I thought your clothes seemed familiar. But how did you get down here?"

"We left our car up the glen," he continued, "and climbed the Buck-ale. After we met you, we traversed the tops and dropped down into Laraig Gartain. Then we climbed the mountain this side of that valley, Buck-ale Etive the other one, and came down into the valley on the other side of the ridge here."

"The Laraig Eilde," I prompted.

"Yes, that's it. Next we went up that peak at the head of the valley here and came down the Bealach Dearg. Cor, what ruddy names these hills have!"

"Well, you've both had quite a day. Sassenachs are usually satisfied with one peak. You've done about six."

"Are you in the rescue team?" white pants asked.

"Yes, but I don't think we have any takers tonight. It was probably just a thwarted lamb trying to milk a late supper."

"I thought in these parts you gave the lost and broken three months' grace before you instigated a rescue," blue jeans said with a laugh.

"We can offer you a little burnt curry," the stirrer put in.

"No, thanks, I'd better be off and make a token search. Anyhow, I have a steak in my pocket." I didn't appreciate the strangeness of my remark until I had departed.

I went up the steep face to Gearr Aonach directly opposite their camp to check out various rock climbs. This base of cliffs is always a likely place to search for both climbers and dropped equipment.

It is customary when a new climb is done to give it a name. Often these are both imaginative and pertinent. Above me

were various routes: Rainmaker, The Wabe, Mome Rath,
Lost Leeper, Minsy, Rev Ted's.

There was still no sign of the mysterious caller, though I
spied a shy herd of red deer. Looking down on the camp I
saw that the two climbers had retreated to the protection of
their tent. By now the evening shadows had climbed the
opposite hillside, giving a uniform mat texture to the west
face of Beinn Fhada.

I spoke to Willie on the radio. "Nothing doing here,
Willie. I had a natter with a couple of lads who are camped
on the flats, but they've seen bugger all."

"Aye, OK, Hamish. Do you want Jim MacKay to come
up? He's here."

"No thanks, I'll be heading back shortly, but you'd better
wait at base till I return."

"Right."

I continued the search on the way along the face skirting
across terraces, but with no result.

"Not a sausage up there, Willie," I reported, back on the
road, "but I guess we'd better get the team out tomorrow
just in case. It's the weekend anyhow, and some exercise will
do us good."

"Well, this won't do," Willie expostulated. A favourite
phrase of his when time is pressing or hostelries open. "I'll
do a call-out for the morning." He chugged down the road in
his Morris Traveller.

Later that evening I 'phoned John Grieve and Denis
Barclay and we discussed the probabilities. Like me, they
felt it was better to have at least a quick check of the Lost
Valley the next day.

It was a soporific morning, already warm, the sort of day
that reminds me of when a crofter was asked if there was an
equivalent to *mañana* in Gaelic. His reply was, "No, there is
no word in the Gaelic which conveys that sense of urgency."
Certainly as we filed into the Lost Valley that Sunday we
weren't bubbling over with enthusiasm or energy.

Inspector Douglas MacCorquodale was at base. He had been Police Sergeant in Glencoe some time before and was now stationed in Oban. Willie and the Police had scoured the glen checking parked vehicles, but all had been accounted for and, due to the uncertainty of the operation, RAF Leuchars were quite understandably reluctant to send over a helicopter to assist us. At base with Douglas MacCorquodale were Willie Elliot and John Grey. John, who was then working at the Clachaig Inn for Rory MacDonald, had taken the truck up. Rory had turned out in his kilt as usual – after all, it was Sunday.

We also had a good representation of the Oban Police. They used to supplement our team in an understanding which we had with the Chief Constable, Kenneth MacKinnon. Our civilian team spearheaded the rescue operation, as we were mainly climbers, and lived locally. By the time we could collect a casualty and start down, the Police would arrive and assist us in the stretcher carry.

That day we had quite a few of the 'regulars': big Jimmy Brown, the Highland policeman with a resourceful Gaelic repertoire, and Sergeant Alasdair MacDougall, a charming man of monk-like serenity; also Alasdair Lynn, then an Inspector and later to become Chief Constable of the Grampian Region.

Denis Barclay caught up with us as we entered the boulderfield. He was as brown as a coffee bean, having just returned from some tropical clime. As well as being ardent skiers, Denis and his wife Iris have an Inca-like infatuation with the sun and scuttle off to exotic strips of sand each year. By some strange quirk of nature, the weather in Scotland is usually delightful for the duration of their holiday abroad.

There were lots of tourists about and some of these ventured up into the Lost Valley. It was even hotter here, as if the wind had never stirred since the beginning of time. Some kids were playing at climbing on the huge boulder which demarks the start of the flat area, and a couple came steaming over the gravel, the man small and the woman extremely fat, her body desperate to escape from her shorts.

We sat down on the grass. After all, it was a long day and there seemed little urgency in our quest. No one had been reported missing, there were no unaccountable cars in the glen and a blank was drawn on all accommodation in the area.

Two smart-looking girls approached, gave us the once-over, then continued across the valley floor. I heard one say, "There must be a rescue!"

Her friend demurely replied, "They don't seem very active, do they."

We weren't then, but we soon would be, as a real-life drama was unfolding just above us.

The rescue team is an interesting group of individuals. Eric Moss, the elderly statesman, an athletic retired Major, adopted rescue work after his first half-century. A former Pipe Major of some renown, he had written a pipe tune a short time before entitled, 'The Glencoe Mountain Rescue Team'. If one was so weak as to partake of a Mars bar on the hill, Eric would fix you in his laser stare and mutter that such pansy luxuries were not available when he was route-marching with the Argylls in India or China. Always one to be on his feet at reveille, Eric was now up and itching to go.

Huan Findlay was there, the local sheep farmer who had played truant on his clippings and brought along a New Zealand sheep-shearer colleague. The family Grieve were in full attendance, all three brothers represented, and even a girlfriend down at base.

On occasions such as this the Police always come in for some stick and, a few days before, there had been a scandal in the Glasgow area where a policeman was remanded for trial on homosexual charges. This, needless to say, was interpreted widely by our local team to include every member of the force. John Grieve warned the boys to be careful of the lawful company they kept on night call-outs.

Will Thomson was lying on the grass with his back propped against a boulder, scanning the cliffs of Gearr Aonach with his binoculars. John and Richard Grieve decided to set off and check the gorge of the Lost Valley stream, while Alasdair MacDougall and the Oban Police contingent were heading higher up the path in the determined footsteps of Major Eric Moss.

The rest of us were attentive to Will, who was describing the moves of several groups of climbers. One party was on a very dangerous section of cliff almost opposite us. As he said later, "I expected one of them to come off, for they were real bumblers." However, another couple to their right were on a climb which I had made about ten years before and which doesn't have a name, but is close to Herbal Mixture, an apt description of the route considering the shrubs thereon. I never did see the first party Will had mentioned, but I saw the other two on what they no doubt thought was Herbal Mixture, but which was a harder climb.

"Christ, he's off!" Will shouted, bounding to his feet. Sure enough, he was. We saw him bounce off a ledge about fifty feet down, then arc outwards until he was brought up short by his rope. He had fallen right down the face and was lying still in a crumpled heap on the steep grassy slope. His second was now high above him, giving the distress signal with his whistle, not realising that we had witnessed the accident.

The team members who had set off heard our shouts or our subsequent radio call. We ran up the face. Will took the lead and kept it, but we were all dogging his heels and arrived breathless at the fallen climber. His mate was still at the stance above, unable to move. We untied the rope of the man who had fallen and examined him. He was critically injured, his head wound, as Will graphically described it, "like an open book".

He was conscious. I asked him, "Can you move your legs?"

He didn't reply right away. Then the awful truth showed in his face.

"No."

He knew he was paralysed. Denis gently cut his laces and eased off his lightweight climbing boots. The rest of us started to build a platform underneath him, for there was danger of him rolling down the slope.

"I'll go down and get the stretcher," Will volunteered, and I radioed base for John Grey or someone to start up with the stretcher and meet Will.

Michael Parsons, the injured man, was now complaining of chest pains. As he was lying face-down, I didn't want to move him unnecessarily because of his spinal injury. However, we had to turn him over in case a rib had punctured his lung, for he was spitting blood. With infinite care we gently eased him over, ensuring that we didn't flex his back a millimetre, and he was instantly more comfortable.

It is the hallmark of good teamwork that you don't have to tell people what to do all the time. As some of the lads were busy with Michael, others had taken care of his friend who had abseiled off the face. As I watched him coming down I suddenly realised that these were the two lads who were camping on the valley floor. So much, I thought ruefully, for their crack about us leaving a rescue search for three months. It's not often the accident is actually witnessed by the team, and we were alongside Michael within fourteen minutes, which must be an all-time record.

I had given Michael Parsons some Fortral tablets, an analgesic, but he was still in agony, though several degrees less than when he was lying face-down. I called Willie.

"Hello, base, come in please."

"Pass your message, Hamish, Willie here."

"Willie, can you ask Douglas to advise Mr Campbell, the surgeon in Fort William, that this lad is seriously injured. Back, ribs and head."

"Aye, OK, Hamish, any idea when you expect to have him down for the ambulance?"

"In about an hour and a half. We'll have to take it easy."

"It's strange," someone said, "this rock being good, that we have such serious accidents on the cliff. Remember that chap and girl who fell in 1968?"

"I remember it well," I replied. "A party from Salford University, trying a new route."

My thoughts took me back to that afternoon when we went up to collect them both. Initially Pamela Higson had fallen, but her friend David Briggs held her. Then she fell again, this time pulling him off his stance. His belay peg came out, and both plummeted over 200 feet, ripping out two peg runners as they fell. Amazingly David only broke an arm and suffered bruising while Pamela had complex head injuries. Her case was a remarkable one from the medical point of view and a television film was made of her subsequent recovery.

I was called back to the present as Will appeared over a crest, and we had the stretcher assembled in two minutes flat. With the team working on a three-two-one command, Michael was lifted and in one smooth motion the stretcher slid underneath him.

Within two hours he was in the Belford Hospital in Fort William being examined by Mr Campbell.

Some months later when Willie Elliot called in he had a newspaper cutting in his hand.

"Isn't this the chap Parsons that we took off Gearr Aonach, Hamish?"

"Yes." I paused, mentally running through rescues on that mountain . . . "The man with the broken back."

"Aye, that's right. He's dead. He committed suicide yesterday."

I scanned the brief news item, then slowly placed it on the table. He had been just twenty-seven.

"In those circumstances, Willie, I think I'd do the same."

7

TWO PLUS TWO MAKES THREE

It never ceases to amaze me how often trivial and seemingly unremarkable incidents can alter the course of life. A friend of mine, George Chisholm, also voiced these sentiments when he wrote to me of the events preceding an accident on the West Face of the Aonach Dubh . . .

"We didn't plan to stay in Glencoe that weekend, as we were to join the Glenmore Climbing Club further north. However, we had a puncture on the way from Edinburgh. The garage at Ballachulish wouldn't do the repair until the Monday, so we stayed in the Glencoe Youth Hostel on Saturday night. To kill time the next day, we traversed the Aonach Eagach Ridge under snow. My friend Fred Mantz assisted me at the awkward descents, as my left knee was troubling me due to an inflammation. In fact, some time later I had to have an operation on it; but otherwise, all went well."

The Glencoe Youth Hostel on a weekend evening in April is a convivial refuge. Climbers and skiers surround the cooking stoves with general anticipation of tomorrow's activities, while the rigours of the present day glow in retrospect.

George and Fred met up with a friend in the hostel on Sunday night, Archie Hannah, there to climb with a young lad from Glasgow. They all decided to join forces for a climb the next day. George, Fred and Archie were old age pensioners, having attained the age of sixty-five, fighting fit, with many routes beneath their climbing boots over the years.

Though they agreed to team up, George certainly wasn't too happy with the arrangement. Both he and Fred had suffered traumatic experiences when joining forces with other climbers . . . One such close shave had happened in Glencoe itself in February 1965. Bidean nam Bian, the peak where the accident occurred, boasts two prodigious northerly buttresses, one in the form of a diamond, the other sporting an elegant arch carefully executed by nature with tunnels and crypts in the basement. Indeed, the buttresses are called Diamond and Church Door respectively and beneath the arch a subterranean rock climb is called the Crypt route. Between these two buttresses, like a gigantic playground slide, lies Central Gully, down which avalanches periodically thunder in dangerous snow conditions. At the base of the gully, between the opposing walls, is Collie's Pinnacle, a rock island or rognon, named after that much-revered pioneer of Scottish climbing, Professor Norman Collie. Here George and Fred joined forces with another couple to climb Central Gully. Fred led and George went second. They didn't belay properly for the gully is not a serious climb – relatively straightforward with crampons.

George recalls: "The snow was hard and my crampons crunched into the firm surface. I used my ice axe as a handhold as I drove it in above me."

One of the other men had a new pair of crampons which didn't fit well and the trouble began when one slipped off his foot.

"Suddenly I felt the rope tighten. One second we were apparently secure on good snow with not a care in the world, and the next we were hurtling down the slope. Of the fall, I have no recollection. I guess we all suffered from shock as we were knocked about. Instead of falling down the right side of the Pinnacle, the way we had come up, we fell down the much steeper left side which has a rock pitch, and then cascaded down the ice below."

With every mishap there is often some redeeming feature which can save the day. In this instance, it was the fact that there was more snow than usual on that particular slope.

Consequently, instead of ugly boulders waiting at the bottom of the climb, a wide snow depression had formed like an enormous white ice-cream scoop. Into this, at high speed, the band of four climbers slid in a jumbled heap of legs, arms, rucsacks and ropes.

When we reached them we were relieved to find three could manage the descent on shanks's pony with a little help from the team, and all would climb again.

Perhaps recollections of this incident went through George's mind as, thirteen years on, he and Fred, Archie and the boy from Glasgow made their way along the narrow road which leads from the Youth Hostel to the foot of Aonach Dubh close to the Elliots' whitewashed cottage. It was one of those three-star mornings which leaves its imprint on the memory cells. Certainly this day, 16th April 1978, will be remembered for ever by George.

As these three elderly climbers and the young man ascended the steep slopes of Aonach Dubh, still undecided on which route they should attempt, I was heading for my garden with resolute steps, bent on a course of action, armed with a can of kerosene and a box of matches.

The previous summer, when I was foolish enough to try to compete with the well-lubricated Highland weed, I had nursed a vegetable garden and I had crow problems. Hoodie crows are probably the most cunning birds in the heavenly kingdom. They are also vehemently hated by shepherds in the Scottish Highlands – and with good reason, I may add. I have witnessed them plucking the eyes from ailing ewes and the tongues from weakling lambs. They zipped open my pea crop and devastated my radishes as though a JCB had worked over them. As a last line of defence, I recruited an ally in the form of a scarecrow. This was no ordinary man of straw, but a work of macabre art.

Having a well-equipped workshop at my disposal, I put together a tall, articulating skeleton of wood and alloy, suitably padded with polystyrene foam and sporting a moulded

plastic head and face of corpse-like pallor. Indeed, everything about it was corpse-like because I had utilised clothing
and equipment from bodies which we had taken off the
mountains over the previous months of rescues. I usually
burn such messy gear, but just then there seemed to be quite
a grisly collection lying in a locker of the rescue truck. The
mangled selection made up the wardrobe of the new garden
guardian: a gore-encrusted helmet, a scree-tattered anorak,
threadbare trousers, a holey pullover and a pair of boots
with one sole missing, all colour co-ordinated – red! At six
feet tall, astride a row of turnips, the scarecrow presented a
daunting and evil-looking apparition. I felt that I had given
birth to a Frankenstein monster. It possessed a frightening
realism, its arms and sometimes even its head moved in the
wind and its painted eye-sockets seemed to embrace every
corner of the garden with an Argus-like vigilance.

A neighbour who took his boy to school each day by car
had a discussion with the lad about the apparently assiduous
tilling of my plot, day after day. Fairly soon, however, the
observant lad pointed out that, if it was me, I hadn't actually
moved position for days! Only on closer inspection did they
realise their mistake! Other friends, upon seeing the tall
garden figure, would bleep their horns to say a cheery hello
and when they got no reaction thought: MacInnes is either
deaf or most unsociable just now.

The scarecrow survived the rigours of the winter and, if
anything, presented an even more unpleasant presence in
the garden as time went by.

It was a fine spring day in April. The cherry blossom was
gay and the sun drenched the hills with a freshness announc-
ing that summer was hot on the heels of spring. Just the day
to make a clean break of it and burn that monster scarecrow,
I thought to myself.

A friend, Dr Morton Boyd, called just as I lit the funeral
pyre. Morton and I had shared days on the Glencoe hills
together. On this idyllic day he had come to photograph a

stately matriarch of a gean, or wild cherry, at my back door, then adorned in delicate spring garb. He greeted me from the depths of his black beard.

"Fine weather, Hamish. I didn't think that I would find you in on such a day."

"Almost didn't, Morton," I returned. "But I had some chores to take care of first. I was just thinking of heading for the tops, but I may have to go anyhow; we'll probably have a rescue. It's been quiet for a week or so." Even as I spoke to Morton the beastly bonfire was crackling enthusiastically in the garden.

"This old tree was supposed to have been here at the time of the Massacre, Morton. What do you think?"

I didn't hear his reply for the 'phone rang, the outside bell, a conversation stopper which amplifies my calls so I can hear them when working about the place. It was Doris Elliot, so I knew it was trouble.

"There's a chap just come in, Hamish. He knows you. Says that his friend has fallen on Aonach Dubh and he's probably dead." Doris pronounced Aonach Dubh as only one born in the Highlands can.

"Where exactly, Doris?"

"It's B Buttress, Hamish."

"OK, Doris, do a call-out, will you? I'll get a chopper."

It was initially up Dinnertime Buttress, the least taxing of the routes on that forbidding West Face, that the four climbers sweated that day. As George said: "I was trailing some hundred yards or so behind, due to my bad knee. The other three had gone round to the right, well above me to the foot of C Buttress, which they tried to climb unroped on the left side. But they gave up and came back towards me to B Buttress. This enabled me to get to the foot of the buttress before them and wait. Fred was carrying a rope over his shoulder. We had both done B Buttress before in summer, but of course now there was still a bit of snow about, even down here. However, instead of taking the ordinary route, we started up to the right, which is easier. Archie climbed a steep rock rib, followed by Fred. The other chap, I can't remember his name, was third. As the walking wounded, I took a rearguard action.

"About thirty feet above, the steep rock gave way to a gentler snow edge which led via another rock step to an expanse of snow. On the right of the snow arête was a vertical rock wall with a groove which Fred had moved into before I got up the snow edge. As I moved upwards, I heard Fred say, 'I'm in trouble.'

"I didn't like to hear that, but I thought, He'll get out of it, and at that moment I was very much involved with the technicalities of climbing, for I was having trouble with my knee.

"A couple of minutes later I was standing alongside the young lad on the snow rib. Archie was above the wall on snow to the left. Fred was stuck in the groove.

"Fred asked Archie if he would give him a hand to support him. The rope, coiled and over his shoulder, had snagged on the rock. But it was too late. Fred slipped backwards, tried to get his feet on a little ledge, overbalanced and fell a hundred feet into the gully on the right. His body landed on snow, but it was sloping and he slithered (unconscious, I hope) several yards and then toppled over the gully wall out of sight. I knew that there was no hope for him. I remember shouting, 'My friend, my friend, he's fallen.'"

When I arrived at the Elliots' house and got out of my car I saw a tall, tired-looking man outside. I didn't recognise Archie Hannah immediately. He had come down to raise the alarm. He told me what had happened and that George was up at the foot of the climb with Fred's body. The young lad was with him. Fred's body was lying on scree in a rock bowl well below Middle Ledge. We didn't say much as we unfolded the stretcher. After putting him in the casualty bag and strapping him on the stretcher we lowered him down the steep face for several hundred feet.

I'd called for a helicopter before leaving base and just as we reached easier ground I could hear the heavy beat of a Sea King chugging high over the Mamores. We took the two back ropes off the stretcher and waited for the helicopter to come in for Fred's last journey from his beloved hills. There was little turbulence and the winching operation went smoothly and when the machine lumbered off all was quiet again. Looking down the valley I could see a thin wisp of smoke rising from my garden.

The sun fired the Aonach Eagach Ridge across the valley in an orange light and the long slit of Clachaig Gully, which rises almost from the bar of the Clachaig Inn, formed a dark scar on the mountainside. Ribbons of snow fingered down from the summits, white and clinical-looking, and as I descended the scree I thought of Fred and how he loved these peaks. He was a bricklayer to trade and a poor man as far as worldly goods are a measure of wealth, but he had a surplus of something far more precious, a contagious enthusiasm for the mountains and a boundless generosity. Every Christmas since his accident on Bidean in 1965, he had never failed to send some donation to the rescue team. Sometimes it was only five shillings he had left over after he had bought his presents. Each year there was always an apologetic note: "Sorry I can't afford more, Hamish, but I know every little bit helps."

I'll always remember Fred as the small quiet man with the big heart.

8

DIY RESCUE

Not all the accidents on the West Face of Aonach Dubh have terminal results. For example, Will Thomson, a staunch team member, who would have been an excellent recruit for Robin Hood's Merry Men, was carried off the hill on one occasion with only a broken leg.

Will used to alternate his tree-felling occupation with climbing instruction, and during the so-called summer of 1978 he had a rock-climbing course with pupils that included an Aberdonian, a Tasmanian and a Londoner. Quite, one would think, the ingredients for a dirty joke. The Londoner was Larry Taylor, who later became a member of our rescue team.

On one particularly wet morning these four climbed to the foot of B Buttress. Everything was saturated. It was the dank soggy weather in which lichen rejoice, oozing fresh slickness to their already slippery coats.

Willie Elliot, with his now somewhat portly, or some would say, stately appearance is the self-appointed guardian of the glen. He is also the officially appointed one, being the National Trust Ranger. He keeps a sharp eye on his flock (sheep) from the many lay-bys on the A82 by means of his trusty brass-bound telescope. But climbers, as well as sheep, sometimes stray into the field of view, and are duly noted. One never knows when such information will come in useful. In fact, we often have to rack our brains about some party we have seen earlier in the day that is reported missing later.

Willie was 'spying' several sheep high on the West Face of Aonach Dubh when he saw the climbers. The leader, a burly figure he recognised as Will Thomson, was spreadeagled on the rock high above the rest of the party who were standing on a rock ledge.

At that particular moment, Will was muttering into his beard about the greasy rock. The day before he had taken his pupils up Agag's Groove on the Buachaille in what he described as "crashing rain". Today was even worse, for here on B Buttress the rock resembled a vertical skidpan. In fact, at the top of the second pitch Will was so disgusted with the condition of the route that he started to climb down. He didn't want an accident with inexperienced pupils and on this trip one was a mere novice. Will describes what happened next.

"Something attracted my attention and, looking up, I saw a bloody great block of rock coming towards me. I thought it must have been loosened by the rain. I desperately swung to one side as fast as I could, but it caught me a glancing blow and bust my thigh. I shouted down to Larry on the stance below, telling him that I had been hit and that I had broken my leg: 'Go down to the Elliots', Larry, and call out the team.'"

"The others weren't experienced enough to help much, so I had to help myself. I climbed out to a rock spike on one side but it wasn't good enough to abseil from so I had no alternative but to climb down. However, I used the spike as a very poor runner and climbed down to join them on the stance at the top of the first pitch. From here I abseiled to the foot of the climb."

This brief, matter-of-fact statement of Will's describes what would be to mere mortals an amazing feat of determination and courage. Larry had already started down and, being adroit at fell running, was the ideal man to recruit help. He bounded down the face as if emulating Will's hostile boulder.

All this had taken time and Willie, at his vigil on the A82 beside his van, was concerned about the inactivity. He hadn't spotted the well-camouflaged boulder dropping down the face, or Larry's mercy dash. He 'de'-telescoped his 'glass', slipped it on to the passenger seat, started his van and cruised home at his statutory 35 m.p.h. for lunch.

When he entered the cottage the matter had almost slipped his mind. After all, he thought, nothing much can happen to Will Thomson – he's indestructable, though he was still half-expecting to see someone arrive for help.

Walter, Willie and Doris were sitting down to their soup when the back door crashed open and Larry ran in, covered in sweat.

"Will's fallen and broken his leg," he reported breathlessly.

"Oh," Walter said, still raising his spoon to his lips, "if it's only Will, there'll be no hurry. Have a plate of soup, Larry."

Larry, who didn't realise for a moment that Walter was teasing him, was flabbergasted, then they all burst out laughing.

The team was quickly mustered, those that were available, and they rushed quickly up to B Buttress. It's not often that we get a chance to rescue one of our own members and the most had to be made of the event.

Will didn't need much help, however. Having got himself down the face unaided he crawled on to the stretcher and grudgingly accepted being subjected to such indignity by directing operations from a sitting position, not the most suitable posture for a broken femur! His subsequent journey must have been quite a revelation to him after having taken hundreds down himself over the years. But he took it in good part. He even took photographs of the operation.

"Hey, Willie Elliot, you watch that bleeding rope, take it over to your left a bit. I don't trust any of you bastards."

Further down, Walter almost joined his sheep-gathering, deer-stalking ancestors, for the mountain, as with the evacuation of the two doctors years before, had to have the last say. As if it hadn't inflicted enough mischief for one day, boulders hurtled down the slope and one the size of the Elliots' twenty-two-inch colour TV missed Walter's head by an aerial's breadth.

Will, as everyone expected, made a lightning recovery, and in a couple of months was back between the stretcher shafts, to which he is more suited. He was not our most docile casualty, but perhaps we were not the most sympathetic rescuers.

9

A DOUBLE FOR THE PARAFFIN BUDGIE

May 1980 was a scorching month. It was the sort of weather which miraculously severs the soggy tentacles of a long winter and woos one with the false impression that it's never been anything else but fine and dandy. The heat had not stopped a number of venturesome souls from taking to the peaks. It was possibly the high temperature which motivated them to sample whatever delicate summit draughts were stirring. I had been working up in north-west Scotland where I gashed my hand badly and had had to resort to a do-it-myself job with needle and cotton as I was in a remote spot. When I returned home the next afternoon, Saturday, 24th May, I was still feeling groggy, certainly not in condition to run up a mountain. But two people had fallen.

It was the morning of 24th May that three young men, Raymond Jefferies, Callum Fraser and Chris Rice, climbed up to Middle Ledge. The previous evening they had pitched camp by the banks of the stream which drops down from Coire nam Beith, not far from the Elliots' cottage. Middle Ledge provides the easiest access for Big Top and other routes on E Buttress. The ledge is an airy horizontal catwalk with the dizzy crags of Aonach Dubh's West Face leaning above and a 'magnetic' come-hither drop on the other side. Only two of these young men were to walk back along Middle Ledge under their own steam. The other would be carried on a stretcher.

Meantime, across the glen on that great northern barrier, the Aonach Eagach Ridge, the narrowest ridge on the British mainland, a party of two was setting off. Lorna Whitelock and Steven Hubball were hill walkers in their twenties from

Cumbria and they intended to traverse the jagged three-mile-long ridge from east to west.

The first scramble was for Lorna. She had fallen 400 feet when descending from the summit crest, above Loch Achtriochtan, and had sustained serious head injuries and severe bruising.

It is a policy with our team to make for the scene of an accident irrespective of whether a helicopter, sometimes known as 'the paraffin budgie', is coming or not. One was, but Ronnie Rodger and Will Thomson perspired up the long relentless slope regardless, Will stripped to the waist and carrying the stretcher. They arrived just before the chopper swooped in.

Lorna was given first-aid and strapped into the stretcher. The winchman clipped the swivel hook on to the four helicopter wires and she rose gently, rotating slowly towards the grotesque yellow belly of the Wessex. It was a slick rescue, but even before she was hauled aboard that aerial platform Will and Ronnie whooped their way down the scree, and about the time Lorna was transferred to a waiting ambulance at the Fort Willam car park which doubles as an emergency helipad Will and Ronnie arrived back at the rescue truck looking like freshly cooked lobsters.

Will's instinct on such occasions is to reach for a can of Guinness, with which we are plied by the manufacturers, and gulp this down as though having just stumbled upon a well-stocked oasis. Walter Elliot has a droll voice and he can often be masterful in understatement. He was the first to break the news. "There's another accident on Big Top, Will . . ."

Quite a few of the team members had arrived at the Elliots' for the first rescue, but hadn't gone up the hill as the helicopter's return was imminent and they knew that Will and Ronnie could handle Lorna's evacuation without difficulty. They were now preparing gear to take up to Big Top.

It was Doris who had got word of this last accident. She'd

contacted Sergeant Cathel MacLeod, who had advised, through the Fort William Police Station, that the chopper was needed again. It was to be refuelled before returning.

Within half an hour it could be seen chugging from the north-west, high over Loch Leven, like a large yellow duck, and then it whirled its way down on to the Elliots' field.

Only Walter Elliot, Will Thomson and Davy Gunn climbed aboard, for it was heavy with fuel. The pilot had told them on the radio that he hoped to land them on the top of E Buttress. Not an easy manoeuvre for he had to keep some power up his sleeve and didn't want to jettison any fuel. They took off and climbed between the opposing faces of Aonach Dubh and the Aonach Eagach Ridge.

The report that Doris got was that a climber had fallen over a hundred feet off Big Top and was hanging on his rope. He had been climbing on two ropes. The other had apparently broken. What actually happened a short time before was this.

Raymond Jefferies from Newton Mearns near Glasgow, a PhD student at Strathclyde University, had been leading on the last pitch of the climb. This section starts easily enough and because of this climbers don't always use the protection of running belays when they are available. Further on, when it gets harder, protection is more difficult to find. It was here that Raymond came off. As he fell, one of his ropes sheared on a sharp edge and parted, but the other held. He was killed when he hit the steep slabs over a hundred feet below.

As the big helicopter made contact with the exposed crest of E Buttress, Walter, Will and Davy jumped out. The machine then took off and descended again while the three rescuers made their way down No 4 Gully which adjoins E Buttress. Walter had a rope with him to fix on any awkward section.

The helicopter started a shuttle service to the top of the buttress, taking three more of the team up, then as the fuel got used, four at a time. Bob Hamilton was on the second trip. Half an hour before he had been an appreciative spectator at the Appin Horse Show. Now he was picking his way down the steep rock in the gully to the bottom of the climb with the folding stretcher on his back.

"I'm certainly glad that some thoughtful person put this rope in place for us," he called to Will Thomson down below.

"Aye," Will replied, "Walter has his uses!"

Meantime, up on the climb seventeen-year-old Callum Fraser and Chris Rice, Raymond's companions, were in an unenviable situation. Chris had managed to pull the suspended body of his friend into the rock face but they couldn't do anything more until they got assistance from the team. Far below they could just discern the minuscule blob of colour which was their tent.

By this time a number of the team had been flown up and Will was now in the gully directly below the scene of the accident. He shouted to Callum and Chris to lower a rope and he would then attach our 500-foot non-stretch rescue rope to it. Then he climbed across to the start of another climb on E Buttress, Trapeze, a route which leads directly up the face to join Big Top close to the crest.

Chris was occupying the same stance that John Grieve and I had used on the Jimmy McDowell rescue eleven years before.

The rope from the two climbers squirmed down the face and when it came within reach Will grabbed it and quickly tied it to the end of the rescue rope.

"OK, haul away."

Will looked across into the gully and saw Bob Hamilton struggling down with the stretcher. He shouted over, "You'd better hurry, Hamilton, or the rescue will be over by the time you get down."

Once the rescue rope was hauled up, instructions were shouted to Callum and Chris to tie the body to the middle of the 500-foot rope. Will tossed an end of this rope to Huan Findlay in the gully. They watched Callum attaching the heavy rope to Raymond's harness and when this was completed one of the team shouted: "Lower the body down now. We have the other end in the gully to guide it."

Though Callum and Chris must have been shocked, they followed these instructions and Raymond's body started its descent. The guide rope, the other half of the rescue rope, was controlled by Huan Findlay and Walter Elliot and the pathetic bundle, which until a short time ago had been a virile young man, was lowered with great precision directly on to the stretcher. Callum and Chris now pulled the 500-foot rope up the face and prepared to use it doubled to abseil.

As soon as the body was secured, the stretcher was taken down the short section of gully to the end of Middle Ledge, for the ledge comes to an abrupt halt when it meets No 4 Gully. The helicopter crew, who were waiting down on the Elliots' field, then got the call to come up. For the lads were confident that the chopper would be able to winch it aboard from here, using the full extent of winch wire.

The helicopter came into view from above and slowly felt its way down towards the jaws of No 4 Gully. As the gully walls rise several hundred feet on either side, it's a tricky operation to ease the machine into a position where it can maintain a hover. That day it was impossible due to down-draughts and turbulence. The pilot's voice came metallically over half a dozen team walkie-talkies.

"Sorry, lads, it's too bumpy in here today, you'll have to move to another position lower down."

It was decided to carry the stretcher along Middle Ledge to B Buttress where the face isn't quite so steep. The sombre cortège moved across Middle Ledge, literally a gripping experience for those on the outside of the stretcher with nothing on their left but bountiful space. Once across on the less abrupt slopes close to Dinnertime Buttress the

Wessex could return and Raymond was winched heaven-
wards. It was a sad end to a fine spring day.

The boys ran down the hillside to slake their thirst in the
Clachaig bar where the owner always stood a free pint to
rescuers. Will and Ronnie had earned two.

10

HARPIC AND A COURAGEOUS MAN

I first saw Harpic across the dining room in Glencoe's Kings-house Hotel at an annual dinner of the Glasgow University Mountaineering Club. I was the guest speaker. Martin Hinde, alias Harpic, was to reply. Martin, who is a crane operator by trade and a madcap by reputation, had been adopted by the Glasgow University Mountaineering Club, or perhaps he had adopted the club, I never knew which. At any rate he was their eccentric mascot. Incidentally, the name Harpic is derived from the catchphrase advertising a well-known lavatory product – hence, 'clean round the bend'. He is a fine climber. Still in his climbing clothes, he entered the dining room that brittle winter's evening, having just returned from completing a hard ice route on Ben Nevis.

The Glasgow University Mountaineering Club, like many such learned bodies of young people, seldom stands on ceremony, and this function was no exception. Though the MC for the night had only a passing acquaintance with Harpic, the latter-day Don Quixote, I witnessed him scoop a half-pound (sorry, 250g) of butter from its pad on the table and press it resolutely into Harpic's right ear. By such actions are memorable evenings created.

23rd August 1981 was a brilliant day – at least the morning was. Kids were splashing in an ankle-deep River Coe, and the retired suntanned brigade were contentedly grilling themselves by their cars on candy-striped fold-away chairs.

A solitary climber, John Melvin Phillips, aged twenty-eight, left the Red Squirrel Camp Site in the lower glen and drove up the A82 to a lay-by opposite the Three Sisters.

These peaks, Beinn Fhada, Gearr Aonach and Aonach Dubh, squat on the south side of the glen like stately matriarchs. Phillips crossed the bridge over the River Coe, just below the Meeting of the Three Waters, and made his way into the confines of the Lost Valley, which sidles between Beinn Fhada and Gearr Aonach. His intention was to climb to the head of the valley and then bear up right to gain the saddle between Bidean nam Bian, the highest peak in Argyll, and its neighbour, Stob Coire nan Lochain. He thought he would probably descend by dropping into the Bidean Coire to follow the stream which eventually bounds past the Elliots' cottage to the valley floor.

He must have been on his way down by the time Harpic and Brian Kelly started up Aonach Dubh. They were climbing the steep bank of the gully on the right-hand side of Dinnertime Buttress, heading for Middle Ledge.

Brian hadn't rock climbed before, and as an introduction Harpic proposed taking him up a route in the Amphitheatre, a vast rock arena which runs out near the top of the mountain and which houses some magical scenery. It's the sort of set Lord Tennyson must have had in mind for 'Blow Bugle Blow'. The weather was hot enough to distract them from their goal, and they lay back soaking in the sun, gazing up towards the Amphitheatre, still high above.

Shortly before Harpic and Brian had taken their ease, and unbeknown to them, Fate had played her cards. John Phillips had descended the west side of Stob Coire nan Lochain and picked his way down the vast no-man's-land of scree towards the top of the West Face of Aonach Dubh. To gain the Bidean Coire he should have borne left. He made his way across the steep ground which constitutes the top of the face, one moment enjoying the fresh air and tramping the bens, the next watching high-speed moving pictures of his life. A handhold had broken when he was crossing the mouth of a rocky scoop, and suddenly he was falling, falling into the upper reaches of No 5 Gully.

In winter the lower part of the gully is known as the Icicle, or Elliot's Downfall. It forms a natural drainage system from the upper face, descending in a series of drops and waterfalls to end abruptly on an overhang like a chin. Here in winter an icicle forms – a translucent column 160 feet high. Needless to say, it is a technically hard and dangerous winter climb, especially during a thaw when it would be possible to fall with the Icicle and jointly disintegrate on the rocks below. On 23rd August there was no ice of course, just a steady cascade of water leaping to freedom.

John's initial fall wasn't that far – relatively speaking. Looking up, he realised that he would never be able to climb back out, and he was also painfully aware of the fact that very few people venture to this area of the mountain during the summer months. He knew there was a great possibility that he could lie there ad infinitum suffering the anguish of a lingering death, and decided that there was no alternative, he would have to go down – down to a point where he could at least shout for help.

Pulling himself down to the next drop and dragging a broken leg, he threw himself over the next pitch. Though he didn't know it he was then on a traverse line which winds round the face and in several hairpin bends leads to a point above our BBC helipad on F Buttress. But even if he had known of this escape route it is still doubtful whether he could have crawled all the way to the edge of the Bidean Coire.

One can but marvel at his singleness of purpose: how he could summon up the courage to throw himself over a cliff edge, just systematically smashing himself to pieces, bit by bit. It was a kind of Russian Roulette in reverse with all chambers but one loaded.

The next drop was sixty feet. He slithered over the edge before crashing down. It is possible that he broke his other leg here and perhaps his back and nose. Where he landed, the gully bed was even more obscured from below than it was from higher up.

Above left, Image intensifiers being demonstrated to the team. HRH Prince Charles later presented us with two on behalf of Rank's and Pilkington. *Above right,* Tiki and Rangi, founder members of the Search and Rescue Dog Association. *Below,* John Stirling lands his Whirlwind on the A82 during a busy rescue day.

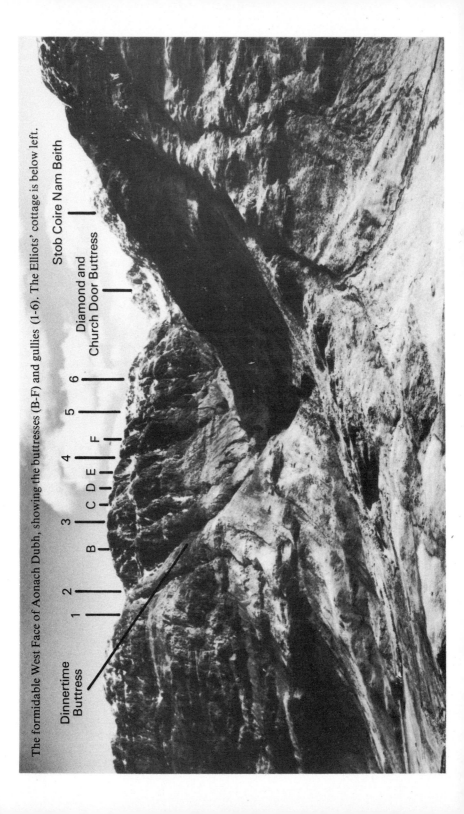

The formidable West Face of Aonach Dubh, showing the buttresses (B-F) and gullies (1-6). The Elliots' cottage is below left.

Some of the team in action: *above left,* Will Thomson and the RAF Leuchars Wessex helicopter; *above right,* Kenny MacKenzie and Echo; *below,* a fatality being taken from the Wessex after a prolonged search in Glencoe. *Left to right,* Willie Elliot, David Cooper, Eric Moss, Sgt Cathel MacLeod, a volunteer searcher, Constable Stuart Obree, the author with back to camera, and the pilot, Steve Murkin.

Left, the approach to Ossian's Cave on the north side of Aonach Dubh. The 'step' below the cave is known as Ossian's Ladder and is 200 feet high. *Above,* Harpic. *Below,* Huan Findlay, Peter Weir and Will Thomson bringing down a casualty from Bidean nam Bian.

Looking across to Gearr Aonach and the Lost Valley (*left*). 1 Lost Leeper, 2 Rev Ted's, 3 McArtney's Gully, 4 Herbal Mixture.

Above, Buachaille Etive Mor from the Glencoe road in winter. *Below,* the author, on the ground, helping evacuate an injured climber on Buachaille Etive Mor.

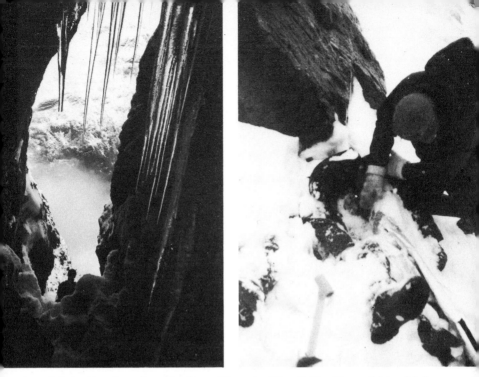

Above left, looking down from the Central Branch of Rev Ted's. *Above right and below,* a sad end to a search for three climbers on Buachaille Etive Mor.

Above, the White Corries chairlift on a normal busy day. Fiona and Guy went right of the right-hand tow in a whiteout. *Below right,* Will Thomson gives Fiona his gloves after she emerges from her avalanche; *below left,* winchman Bob Danes brings Guy in to base.

It is difficult to know how long he lay there, but it couldn't have been more than half an hour, for it was about 3.30 p.m. that Harpic and Brian heard what they thought initially was the bleating of a sheep. They decided to go further across the slope to investigate.

A waterfall nearby was partially masking the cries. As a matter of fact the pitiful calls could be heard by people outside the Clachaig Inn on the valley floor over a mile away and 1000 feet below. Others who heard the cries thought they sounded like the roaring of a stag. But it was neither sheep nor deer, but a man in agony, calling for his life to be saved – time was literally running out.

Meanwhile Harpic and Brian had found a sheltered scoop which shielded the sound of the water and they could now distinctly hear cries for help. As Harpic told me later: "I just couldn't pinpoint it, so I climbed a bit higher on my own. I felt that the cries came from somewhere between No 5 and 6 Gullies, but the area of the face is vast, steep and vegetated with lichen-covered rock. I thought the calls were coming from above where the Icicle forms in winter in No 5 Gully, certainly from that region."

Harpic turned round and shouted, "Brian, there's some-one hurt all right. Go down for the rescue team and I'll try and climb up to him." Brian hurtled off as befitted the matter of life or death it was.

Harpic said afterwards, "I realised that it had been a serious accident, for there was a pathetic tone to the calls, and there's no way of simulating such cries of distress. I scouted round the bottom of the face to see how I could get up. The cliff over which the Icicle spills was out of the question. Not only is it overhanging for about 160 feet, but it is also greasy and hanging with moss. There was a line to the left, the ramp of a winter route which leads into the gully above the top of the Icicle, but this patch looked highly dangerous, the sort of place where a dedicated botanist could perish in pursuit of his profession. I took my rucsack

off and left it on top of an orange bivvy bag at the base of
No 5 Gully. I thought it would provide a marker for the
rescue team. I then worked over to the right towards No 6
Gully and just before the deep trench of this I found a line
which took me up to a sloping ledge system. Without hesitat-
ing I resolved to attempt this."

Harpic doesn't say much about that climb, but it must
have been frightening even for the experienced mountaineer
he is, used to hard solo climbing. He dismissed it, saying:
"Sometimes you must make decisions without thinking of
the consequences." It is perhaps true to say that in both war
and peace such action is the essence of outstanding bravery.

He had traversed across the grassy ledge which nearly, but
not quite, connects the two gullies. A blank area of rock
prevents access to the end of this from the top of where the
Icicle starts.

"I abseiled from a couple of chocks and found him on the
edge of the steep section where the water from No 5 takes its
160-feet plunge. I called to him as I got nearer and could
hardly believe my ears when he croaked that he had fallen
from the top of the face. I had to jump from the end of
the rope across and into the gully. Once there, I looked the
injured man over. He wasn't a pretty sight, with a broken
nose and multiple bruises. His lips were swollen and purple.
He presented the sort of picture which would give the faint
of heart a coronary. Indeed, he looked as if he had spent the
afternoon in a refuse compressor. One leg was hanging as if
it didn't have a rightful owner. I adjusted it, putting it back
where it more or less belonged, until someone more skilled
than I could attend to it.

"He told me that he had thrown himself over the pitches
and that he had decided to give himself another half-hour at
this one, before committing himself. That final plunge on
to the rocks below would certainly have killed him. But the
pain, he said, was so intense that he couldn't take it much
longer."

The sun of early afternoon was replaced by a damp blanket of cloud and, as one would expect, the temperature dropped.

"We talked. He was convinced that he was going to die, and by the look of his injuries this appeared a reasonable deduction. But I tried to cheer him up by saying that the team would be here shortly and he would soon be off to hospital. Time passed slowly. I felt chilled but had little to complain about when judged alongside my gory companion."

Meanwhile, down in the valley, the wheels of rescue had started to grind when Brian arrived at the Elliots'. After establishing the facts with her usual thoroughness, Doris reached for the 'phone.

RAF Pitreavie in Fife, which is the Air/Sea Rescue Co-ordinating Centre, promised that a Wessex which was in the area would divert to the scene. However, due to the descending cloud, it never made it to the West Face. Peter Weir and Ronnie Rodger were first on the scene, taking the normal path up towards Coire nam Beith, which is an offshoot of Bidean Coire, past the leap-for-joy waterfall known to the tourist trade as Ossian's Shower. Indeed, had that bard lived in the nearby grotty cave which bears his name, such forceful ablutions would be necessary. This point affords a good view of the West Face of Aonach Dubh across the stream. As they ascended they could hear the calls, and higher they spotted Harpic at the top of the Icicle pitch.

They shouted, saying that they were coming up. However, they were not sure how to get into the place and rightly went further into the corrie so that they could then double back along the south end of Upper Ledge to a point above Harpic.

Most of the team had converged on the Elliots' field by now, and several parties were making their way up the steep slopes towards the gully. The trouble now was that darkness was seeping into the glen, flooding the lower reaches like a black tide, whilst above, the cloud had sunk even lower, depressed by its own weight.

Between, in the middle of the crepuscular sandwich, were Bob Hamilton, who had the heavy 500-foot Speleo rope on his back, and just ahead, John Grieve and Ed Grindley. Like Ronnie and Peter, John's party made contact with Harpic, yelling into the mist. Sounding unreal and remote, they heard Harpic shout, "I think I'm at the point where the Icicle starts."

They, too, decided to reach the accident spot via the end of Upper Ledge. This would at least get them easily to a point a few hundred feet above where Harpic and John Phillips were patiently waiting.

John got on to the walkie-talkie and tried to contact the next party behind, but was unable to raise them. He wished to tell Denis Barclay to wait at the bottom of No 5 Gully, as it was most likely that this was the way they would have to do the evacuation.

It was almost dark now and team members in twos and threes followed John and Ed up to the traverse line. Here Ronnie and Peter met them. As Denis sweated up the steep boulder-strewn slope, his headlamp fingering the night, he came across Bob struggling with his burden, the 500-foot rope. Denis relieved him of this and they both carried on to the point where Upper Ledge cuts across the gully, where John's party were awaiting the long rope. John Phillips must have either fallen over, or crawled across here for his next plunge.

John Grieve, tongue in cheek, asked Denis, "What the hell was keeping you with that rope?"

Mike Hall, who had run most of the way up the hill, came charging round the ledge. Due to a corner of jutting rock, he didn't see the others until he was almost on them.

"Oh!" he exclaimed. "I wasn't sure where you were."

"Neither are we," some wag responded.

The boys still weren't certain that Harpic and the casualty

were at the top of the Icicle. Harpic thought they were, but it was difficult to tell in the dark.

The team now moved to the edge of the gully, avoiding John Phillips's rapid descent line. This took them to a subsidiary rock chimney which forms a natural route behind a large chockstone, known as the Needle's Eye. They stood on top of the minibus-sized boulder and shouted. A responding cry came from below.

"We're down here – to your left." The headlamps swung round to the source of sound and came to rest. There, about eighty feet below, in the pool of light and in a mass of blood, were two figures.

"We'll be with you shortly," John shouted.

Ronnie set up an abseil while Ed borrowed Mike Hall's harness and John Grieve, Denis's. Both prepared to make the diagonal descent into the gully, not an easy manoeuvre in darkness, but the team didn't have a searchlight at this time and personal headlamps don't illuminate the rock beneath one's feet too well.

As he was going down John suggested that everyone except Ronnie and Bob should go back along the ledge and return to the bottom of No 5 Gully, as a cableway would most likely have to be used with the bottom end of it anchored down there. This aerial ropeway would have the stretcher attached on it by two pulleys and would have to be lowered on a separate rope. The stretcher had already come up the hill and was now at the bottom of the gully.

Harpic felt almost as relieved to see the descending figures as did the casualty. He recognised a shining head gleaming in torchlight as Ed approached. (Like others in the team, Ed would have appreciated a more generous growth on his skull.)

"Hi, Ed."

Ed swung his lamp round over the grisly scene. "Oh, it's you, Harpic. What are you doing here?"

The weather had really socked in like cold pea soup. By

this time John Phillips had stopped bleeding. But it was an eerie scene, especially from above: blood-crusted rocks and, just in front of Harpic, a short dip then jet-black nothingness.

John and Ed had a discussion as to the best way to evacuate the casualty. Ed advocated keeping him there till morning, well wrapped up, while John was all for lowering him pronto to the bottom of the gully. John's proposed course of action of getting him on to "terra a little more firma" as soon as possible was adopted.

The team may curse and blind and appear sometimes oblivious to suffering, yet when there's a job in hand, someone in genuine trouble, they work like efficient automatons. Each knows what he's good at and does it. There was no discussion as to who was to administer first-aid that night or who was to fix the cableway evacuation. John Grieve immediately got to work studying the rocks for cracks for peg anchors, and Ed, who has a passion for advanced first-aid, metaphorically rolled up his sleeves. It was the sort of situation that every ardent first-aider dreams of.

Up on the Needle's Eye Ronnie was preparing to descend. John Grieve had asked for more manpower.

"Which is the best way down here, Walter?" Ronnie asked. "Over or through the Needle's Eye?"

"Oh," Walter responded, "you'd better go through like the camel, Ronnie. There are some sharp rock edges on the lip otherwise, but don't worry, the belay's fine."

Willie Elliot was operating base in the truck close to his cottage. We had obtained this three-ton ex-Army vehicle from the Scottish Home Office some time previously. Willie was relaying messages to various parties on the hill as most were out of line of sight of each other and therefore the reception wasn't too good. Bob, with the others at the top of the Needle's Eye, got a message from John Grieve via Willie asking for the 500-foot rope to be thrown down.

"I'm not sure I quite understand that," Bob said to the

others sharing the lump of rock. "I'd better ask again, this could be a do or die situation."

He had heard correctly and proceeded to heave the rope into the spot of light below.

"OK, got it." A shout drifted up from the puddle of light.

As Ronnie did his crab-like abseil into No 5 Gully, the remainder of the party set off for the bottom of the Icicle pitch; Walter, in the lead, scuttled along the exposed ledge as if closing time at Clachaig bar was imminent.

Meantime, back with the casualty, Ed did better than all the King's Men of Humpty Dumpty fame, and John Phillips was assembled as well as could be expected in the circumstances. As he did so Ed must have been recalling an incident a few months earlier when one of my stretchers had been returned by the Department of Health for Dunbartonshire, after being used to evacuate a Hepatitis B victim, injured in the mountains near Arrochar. The stretcher had arrived minus webbing and net bed which had been incinerated because of possible contamination. Hepatitis B is highly contagious and can be transmitted when the carrier's blood is in contact with that of someone else. Ed had just cut his hand on the abseil. He asked John Phillips half-jokingly: "You don't have hepatitis, do you?"

"As a matter of fact, I do."

"Which type?"

"B, I think."

In the bottom party, dressed in waterproof 'gowns' made from black dustbin liners with holes for arms and heads stood Davy Gunn and John Main. John, a doctor, had been barman at the Clachaig Inn during vacations in his student years. They presented an odd sight perched shivering on boulders close to the bottom of the waterfall, looking like the last of the Ten Little Niggers miserably awaiting their fate.

This medical news was relayed to John Main by walkie-talkie. But as he said, there wasn't much one could do about it, and anyhow it was later established that John Phillips had suffered from Hepatitis A, the non-contagious variety.

Two 150-foot abseil ropes were joined and one end was thrown over the waterfall to the party below. The casualty bag was then tied to it, but it stuck firmly in a crack en route to the top party. It just wouldn't budge. Ronnie volunteered to abseil down and free it, then carry on down to the bottom of the face. The 500-foot rope was lowered over the edge and secured to the good anchor which John Grieve had obtained in the nether regions of the gully. This rope came through a fairlead to get it on the right line for Ronnie's abseil, and also for later use with the cableway.

John belayed Harpic, who went to the lip of the overhang and checked the end of the rope down to Denis Barclay who was with John Anderson, Walter and the rest of the gang below, busy commiserating with each other on the humidity and from time to time doubling up in laughter at some dirty joke.

Ronnie attached a safety rope to his climbing harness, Ed belayed him. He swung over the edge and was barely in contact with the rock when he reached the casualty bag. It was wedged into a shallow crack. He shouted for a tight rope and tried to free it. At first it refused to budge, then it popped out like a champagne cork, and John Grieve, who was pulling like mad on this rope, felt it free, and quickly hauled it to the top of the pitch.

"OK," Ronnie shouted, "I'll go on down now."

He corkscrewed directly under the water which splattered off his helmet. From below in the light of the torches the rope couldn't be seen and he looked a weird sight, an aquatic Peter Pan descending to a drenched stage.

At the bottom, he stood aside and shouted up: "Thanks for the safety rope, lads."

"Yes, Ronnie," a disembodied voice reached him from above, "but we won't have a bloody safety rope when we come down . . ."

The end of the 500-foot rope was anchored at the bottom, out from the wall and tensioned. This now formed the high-angled cableway for John Phillips's evacuation. To take up the stretcher, karabiners were attached to its slings and these were clipped to the taut cableway so that the stretcher was suspended. The tail of Ronnie's safety rope was then tied to the top end of the stretcher. From the bottom Mike Hall shouted to John Grieve, "Take the stretcher up."

John Phillips was already in the casualty bag and he was now eased on to the stretcher and secured. Ed, Harpic and John moved the stretcher to the edge of the short drop which led to the lip of the main overhang. Here it jammed and Harpic, belayed, climbed down to free it. He managed to kick it over the edge into the dark void, the act orchestrated by a drum roll of falling stones.

Once suspended on the cableway, the lights from below picked out the stretcher and like a well-rehearsed stunt it ran smoothly down the cableway.

When it reached the rock below, John and Ed dropped the lowering rope to the bottom of the face. The rescue party were cold with waiting at the bottom for many hours and lost no time in unclipping the stretcher and setting off for the valley floor.

A pained voice reached them from the dark cliff above: "Will some bastard stay with the radio? We've got to bloody well get off."

"Ah, dinna fret," someone shouted back, "ye can always come doon the morrow."

John Anderson agreed to stay to see the three rescuers off the face.

"The 500-foot rope is free now, lads. You can adjust it for abseiling."

'Right," John Grieve called back. "Let me know as I pull it in when the tail-end of it just leaves the bottom. Then I'll chuck the other end down so that we can descend on it doubled."

"Aye, all right."

In ten minutes the other end whistled down; there was enough rope.

The next thing John Anderson saw was a figure, drenched and muttering. It was Harpic, receiving the high-pressure water treatment. He eventually made it, shivering and soaked to the skin. Ed and John Grieve followed then pulled down the end of the long rope. It whizzed down beside them. They quickly coiled it and John Grieve handed it to Harpic.

"Here, Harpic, take this and let's go."

Bleeding Hell, thought Harpic, you just can't win with this Glencoe bunch. And weighed down with his soggy load, he ran down the mountainside in pursuit of the fast-disappearing headlamps of John and Ed.

11

STORM FORCE

I recognised Willie Elliot's voice immediately. There was no preliminary chat; he launched straight into his piece.

"Jean MacLeod 'phoned this forenoon at eleven o'clock. Cathel was away at a road accident on the Rannoch Moor, so she couldn't contact him. She says two boys are missing from Hugh McColl's bunkhouse and that they left at 'an unknown hour'. Their gear is still there and it's not even known if they came back last night or not. They've a red Ford Capri. So I've been up the glen and found it at the Devil's Staircase lay-by."

"What do you think? Any note in it?"

"No, not a thing."

"Climbing gear?"

"No, it seems empty."

"It doesn't look too good with this weather we've been having, Willie. Can you check Glen Etive in case they've gone down from the south side of the glen, and I'll ask the Police to trace the owners on the computer." I paused in concern. "You know, Willie, we'll have to find out if they're climbers or walkers, otherwise where the hell do we look?" As I put down the 'phone I had an uneasy feeling. The weather during the past nine months of 1982 had been thirty per cent wetter than normal and we had had the worst winds in living memory. Each gale or storm seemed to follow hard on the heels of the last. This weather pattern wasn't confined to the west coast of Scotland; all over the world normal weather patterns had been disrupted. I recalled the previous day: it had been a dry morning and there was less snow than normal for January, the time when we usually get heavy

snowfalls in the Glencoe region. The day seemed promis-
ingly fair, had one not heard the shipping forecast; storm-
force winds had been predicted and materialised at noon.
I had been down the coast in Oban that morning and had
seen the angry clouds mustering to the south-west like
sinister wads of guncotton. By one o'clock, when I was back
in Glencoe, horizontal sleet blattered against the window-
panes.

These recollections made me distinctly worried, so by the
time I picked up the telephone to contact the Police, I had
already thought about calling out the rescue team. I spoke
now to Cathel MacLeod, the local Police Sergeant, who had
returned from the traffic accident on the Moor of Rannoch.
Cathel has been a friend of mine for many years, long before
he was posted to Glencoe. As well as being a charming man,
he is a fine athlete and regularly competes in the heavy
events in Highland games: tossing the caber and putting the
shot.

"Hello, Hamish." His voice has a rich Highland timbre.
"Don't tell me there's trouble on a day like this?"

"Could be, Cathel. Willie's found a car at the bottom of
the path at the Devil's Staircase. It's been there all night.
Your wife probably told you about the missing men."

"That's right. I saw it, too. I was up the road a wee while
ago and saw a maroon-coloured Ford."

"Can you check it out, Cathel," I asked, "and find out
where the owner comes from?"

"Sure, I'll do that right away, Hamish."

"Half a mo – see if you can establish if the owner is a hill
walker or a climber. That at least will give us some clue
whether to search a mountain or the open country to the
north."

From where the car was parked the Devil's Staircase toils
up to 1600 feet on the shoulder of Stob Mhic Mhartuin, then
descends to Kinlochleven on the far side of the ridge. The
Staircase is an old military road built by General Caulfield

for the pacification of the Highlands after the 1745 Rebellion. The Redcoats came over this track too under orders from the Master of Stair for the Massacre of the MacDonalds of Glencoe. Their orders were to block off any escape from the glen to the east and south. It was common practice for walkers, even in midwinter, to use the Staircase to head for the remote country to the north and east of Kinlochleven; there they would perhaps camp for a day or so and often didn't leave word of their itinerary.

There was the other possibility that the car owner and his companion had taken the wide sweeping glen, the Lairig Gartain, which leads south to Glen Etive, a walk which any agile grandmother could tackle with alacrity in the spring, but in a winter blizzard it can sap one's strength like the loss of blood. Another alternative was the car had broken down and that the owner and his pal had hitched a lift back home without telling anyone. However, this possibility was unlikely as there were still some belongings left at the bunkhouse. The most serious alternative was that the mystery driver and his companion had gone up Buachaille Etive Mor, the mountain which stands like a heavyweight wrestler at the eastern portals of Glencoe, above the desolation of the Moor of Rannoch. The Buachaille is a mountain of considerable proportions, comprised of solid rock rhyolite, which in the early-morning light of summer makes it resemble the cliffs of Petra. In winter the Buachaille is a more serious proposition in its white shroud. Gullies not so obvious in summer seam its flanks and ice-covered towers promise challenge and joy to the alpinist and chills to flatlanders progressing furtively along the A82 at its base.

On that day, 10th January 1983, the Buachaille was huffing and puffing in a foul temper behind snow clouds; only the lower slopes were visible and the prospect of searching the faces and gullies was unpleasant to say the least.

Time was moving on. At this latitude of 56 degrees north, it gets dark at 4 p.m. in January, even earlier in angry weather, yet I wanted to hear from Willie in Glen Etive before making a move, just in case he had found the missing party.

The 'phone rang again. It was Hugh McColl, who owns the bunkhouse across the river from where I live. He told me that there were actually three men who had not returned.

"Did they have a maroon-coloured Ford?" I asked.

"Yes, I think that's right, Hamish. I've looked to see what gear they left; their sleeping bags and personal items are still here. I've locked the bunkhouse, now," he added, "so if they come back they'll have to come up to my house for the key to get in and I'll let you know if they do."

"Fine," I returned. "Do you happen to know if they're climbers or walkers, Hugh?"

"I didn't see any climbing gear, Hamish." He sounded thoughtful. "But I'll have another look and ring back if there is anything."

"Thanks."

Meantime, Cathel MacLeod had been busy; he had opened the car with Police keys and found a deadman in the boot. This is not a corpse, I hasten to add, but a deadman belay plate, a flat plate of aluminium alloy with a wire sling attached to the centre and a loop at the end to tie on to. It is used by climbers in soft snow for belaying. You insert it in the snow above your stance and pull it down cross-wise into the snow cover so that it provides a large surface anchor which can take a loading of several thousand pounds.

This was a positive clue and now I felt justified in concentrating the search on Buachaille Etive Mor. If they had a deadman belay, they obviously did some winter climbing and the Buachaille is the obvious choice from the Devil's Staircase lay-by.

I 'phoned up Doris Elliot to arrange a team call-out.

"Oh, hello, Hamish." Her familiar lilting voice greeted me. Doris, like her late mother, is as unflappable as a saint, often relaying the most distressing news with calm and equanimity. "I suppose it's about the people in that car up at the Devil's Staircase, Hamish?"

"It is, Doris. Can you call out the team? We'll meet at Altnafeadh at 1.15 p.m. And can you ask John Grieve to take the rescue truck up?"

"Right, Hamish." Her voice was calm and efficient.

Our rescue truck, an ex-Army three-ton four-wheel-drive vehicle, with a large cabin on its back, could perhaps be unkindly mistaken for a mobile canteen or even a Black Maria. As a matter of fact, it did appear briefly as such in *Monty Python and The Holy Grail*. The truck makes an excellent centre for operations and also provides shelter when coming from a rescue. It seems inevitable that the most difficult rescues happen in the worst possible weather. The scene was now obviously set for a Buachaille epic with all of nature's special effects on hand.

The call-out was fast and as I arrived half an hour later at Altnafeadh quite a few of the team were already there. I told the lads the little that I knew of the missing men. There was now no sign of the mountain except for the lower slopes as a mass of truculent clouds had descended like a lowered ceiling.

"It's a fine day for avalanches," I said to Paul Moores, who, at six foot four, is the tallest member of the team. Paul is recognised as one of the country's leading mountaineers at the present time, having taken part in several Himalayan expeditions, and is an indispensable team member.

"We'd better take the bleepers with us today," someone said. There was a general grunt of agreement. Conditions such as prevailed on the mountain just then were the most hazardous rescuers could encounter, with unstable snow which could avalanche at any time. Your chance of survival in a wet snow avalanche is only minutes unless you are very lucky indeed. At least with an electronic bleeper in your shirt pocket you had a hope.

We decided to shift operations a mile up the road to a

larger car park, which is directly beneath the mountain. Just below us several deer were scraping at the soft snow in an effort to find some late lunch. Already quite a few beasts had been dying due to the prolonged spell of bad weather.

A white Police Range Rover swung in behind us, and Cathel wound down the window. "I've had a lot of trouble finding out if the missing men are climbers, Hamish. It seems as if they are really hill walkers, but do a little climbing. I understand they are well equipped. We're having difficulty in contacting the parents of the car owner, but all three men work for an oil company in Glasgow."

"Thanks, Cathel, that is a help, at least. Can you contact Fort William on your radio and request a helicopter? I doubt if they'll come over in this lot," I jerked my thumb in the direction of the hooded Buachaille, "but it's worth a try."

Most of the team had their gear sorted out now and were collecting walkie-talkies and bleepers from the truck.

"Any special preference for where to go?" I asked.

"The pub," some wag retorted.

"All right, then. How about Paul and Jim heading up towards D Gully Buttress, then skirting round past Central Buttress from there?" This was Jim Morning's first call-out with the team. Like Paul, he is a climbing instructor with the Army base at Ballachulish. "Ian, could you go up with Richard Grieve and Ronnie Rodger to the bottom of Curved Ridge? Have a check to see if there are any prints still visible; it looks as if there could be some from here."

Meantime, Willie was back and was now studying the mountain with his trusty telescope. I asked him if he had had any success.

"Nobody in Glen Etive, Hamish."

"Thanks, Willie."

"Hamish?" It was Jim Morning. "That's the RAF team heading south. Will I run and stop them?"

I hesitated for a second, knowing that there could be friction between the RAF Mountain Rescue Team and our

own boys, but the urgency of the situation prevailed and I
said, "Sure, if you can."

He ran up to the main road and succeeded in signalling
the convoy to stop. In a few minutes the Land-Rovers and
three-ton trucks rolled into the lay-by. At least we now had
reinforcements.

John Grieve came over. "I'll go up Great Gully with Davy
Tod. OK, Hamish?"

"Fine."

"Everyone back by dusk or four o'clock," I shouted. "We
can't do much today, anyhow."

"That ruddy river's high," Richard Grieve observed. I
hadn't realised the fact until he pointed it out, but the River
Coupal, which snakes round the base of the Buachaille, was
almost in spate, and the stepping stones covered.

"Pity you didn't take your dry suit, Richard," I remarked.
Both he and his brother John are professional divers as well
as keen climbers.

The remainder of the team were divided in searching the
eastern aspect of the mountain, the Glen Etive side.

John Grieve, Davy Tod, Bob Hamilton and Paul Williams,
as well as some of the others, decided to return to Altnafeadh,
where we had originally parked. Here there was a bridge
which, as well as leading to the normal access path to the
climbs on Buachaille Etive Mor, was also the route off the
mountain via Coire na Tulaich.

"I think that avalanche at the foot of Great Gully is an old
one, Willie, don't you?" I asked.

"It looks like it," he agreed, putting down his telescope.
"It's a wee bit dirty, as if it's been settling for a while, though
I don't remember seeing it a couple of days ago when I was
spying up here."

"Anyhow," I returned, "John and Davy will give it a good
going over, though I don't relish the thought of being in
Great Gully today."

"I had a look up Coire na Tulaich," Willie continued.

"There were five people and a dog heading up towards the summit of the Buachaille. Some folks seem to revel in going out in bad weather."

"They must have something in common with these masochists who get a thrill out of being bound in chains and whipped," I replied. But my thoughts took me back to Great Gully. I had many recollections of near disasters to team members in this great gash, the rubbish tip of the Buachaille. Indeed, two of my friends died in it.

Meantime, Mick Taylor, the Flight Sergeant in charge of the Leuchars Mountain Rescue Team, had his chaps organised. After establishing that we needed his assistance, he set about arranging accommodation for his team for the coming night. They had been helping the Lochaber Mountain Rescue Team search for two Irish climbers who had gone missing in a blizzard some days before (they were not found until the following summer) so most of his team were tired and their clothing was saturated. From his radio truck he had established that the helicopter would arrive in half an hour.

I leant inside the back of this vehicle to give him an outline of the situation. "Where do you want my boys to search, Hamish?"

"As they haven't got avalanche bleepers, Mick, it would be as well if they could concentrate on the easy route down from the mountain on the Glen Etive side; some of our lads are heading there now – Denis Barclay, John Anderson and Peter Weir. If you can search to the south of them; they're going up by the Chasm."

"Right, anywhere else?"

"Yes, Coire na Tulaich, and we're calling off at dusk," I added.

The crowd of rescuers had now thinned, as most of the RAF lads had headed off in trucks to their starting-off points. Across the river we could see the black figures of the Glencoe team making their way laboriously through the soggy snow. The scene was uninviting, sinister. Someone had mentioned, before setting off, that accidents seem to come in threes. We had never had three climbers killed together in Glencoe before and I put the thought out of my mind. Sometimes two are killed together; more often one of a pair survives and can summon help.

The arrival of Mike Hall, one of our team members, dragged me from my morbid thoughts. "Sorry I'm late, Hamish, just got back from a job."

"There's plenty out, Mike, but you can go up in the chopper if you want; it's due to arrive shortly. It's a Wessex, coming over from Leuchars." Leuchars is the usual RAF station that assists us in rescue work, but sometimes we do get the Sea Kings from Lossiemouth, to the north and east. Just as we were speaking we heard the distinctive throb of the aircraft muffled by the cloud and wind. The RAF boys set off a ground smoke-flare to give the pilot wind direction.

It is interesting to see how, over the years, the novelty of helicopter flying has worn thin with team members. Initially, there is the excitement of winching on to some isolated ledge or ice slope where you are often spinning like a top at the end of the wire. But many rescues are enacted in bad weather and it's in winter that the helicopter and its crew are frequently flying close to their limits This usually gets through to the aspirant team member after a few call-outs and he then appreciates the value and the relative stability of his own two legs. The rescue helicopters have a remarkable safety record, which reflects on the ability of those who fly and maintain them. They are very much part and parcel of the modern rescue scene, absorbing much of the hard physical grind of an operation.

All conversation ceased once the large machine poised over the lay-by. Smoke billowed out to windward from the flare and our fluorescent wind marker now pointed away from the downwash of the machine instead of favouring the gale.

"How about Mike Hall and yourself going up?" I shouted to Mick Taylor, the RAF Team Sergeant. "Have a look for any prints above the team."

A few minutes later Mick and Mike were aboard and the Wessex defied gravity once more, rocking towards the mountain like a homeward-bound drunk. It was not a good day for flying and I was glad that I wasn't with them. The sheer scale of the mountain dwarfed the large machine.

There wasn't a great deal of visible ground to cover, for the team members were well up by this time and of course the helicopter couldn't penetrate that dangerous cloud. In such poor visibility the pilot loses all sense of scale and it is impossible to get a fix on anything to enable him to hover or move with safety.

John Grieve and Davy Tod, followed by Bob Hamilton and Paul Williams, had taken the normal access route up the mountain from Altnafeadh. Bob and Paul started searching diagonally upwards. John and Davy went on to the edge of Great Gully and first inspected the avalanche which we had spotted from below. It was an old one and had been there for several days. They then continued upwards, whilst Bob and Paul worked over the face to join them at a point higher up.

Ian Nicholson came on the radio: "Hamish, these prints round the bottom of Curved Ridge seem a bit old. There's nothing fresh here, we've had a good look."

"Thanks, Ian. Keep in touch if you find anything."

Ian, Richard Grieve and Ronnie Rodger had spread out across the face to conduct their search and were now about halfway up the mountain. Paul Moores and Jim Morning had found a big avalanche tip further to the east of Ian's group and had searched this, but there was no sign of anyone buried beneath it. Further round the mountain at the Chasm Denis Barclay, John Anderson and Peter Weir had reported negatively. There just didn't seem to be a trace of humans having been on the hill for days, but probably high winds and drifting snow had obliterated any sign of prints.

Later, I heard again from John Grieve. By this time he and Davy had climbed higher up the edge of Great Gully and Bob Hamilton and Paul Williams were now just behind, having worked obliquely across to where John and Davy were searching. At a particularly exposed part of the gully edge they were assailed by a gust of wind with the kick of a piledriver. Bob was almost hurled into the ice gully below, but just managed to stay attached to the steep ice, using his ice axe, though he slipped down about five feet. His first reaction was, I hope Paul's all right. Paul, just behind him, had managed to stay put as his ice axe had a good placement. It was strange, they thought, for up until then, there in the shadow of the gully, it had been relatively calm. John had also been nearly blown away in the blast.

I heard nothing about this back at base, but John came on to the RT some fifteen minutes later, when they had climbed to a point where an ice pitch has often given us rescue employment in the past. Climbers frequently get stuck or avalanched on this long, but relatively easy section.

"Hamish, Davy and I are thinking of going up the side of Great Gully to the top and down Coire na Tulaich."

I paused for a moment before replying. "Well, John, there's not much time; we'll be recalling everyone shortly."

"That's all right," he replied. "We've got headlamps."

"It's up to you, John, just advise us on what you're doing." After some time, he called back to say that they had decided to return to base.

The helicopter returned to base too, but first it landed down by the river, which I thought was peculiar. The flying conditions couldn't have been worse, with winds of hurricane force higher up and a great deal of turbulence.

"We seemed to fall out of the sky," Mike explained later. He thought the pilot just had to get on terra firma for a few minutes to steady his nerves. It was flying of the highest order and he had made several attempts at landing Mick and Mike on the summit without success. Little did we know it then, but they must have passed within a couple of hundred feet of the missing climbers.

A dank dusk seemed to press down physically from the clouds and Will Thomson, one of our most experienced rescuers, arrived. Will is a competent climber and has been rescuing with us since those dark days when team members pensioned off their wellington boots. He had been away in Fort William that day.

"It's a bit late," he said cheerfully, as he started out. "But I need some exercise, anyhow."

One of the RAF lads brought a hill walker into the base truck. He had found a rucsack. I asked him about it.

"I was just going up the easy way from Altnafeadh, Coire na Tulaich, isn't it?"

"Correct."

"I saw five people up ahead, with a dog."

"Yes, one of our team saw them too," I told the lad.

"Well, I was almost at the final slopes leading to the top of the corrie when I saw a rucsack, a blue Karrimor. It was propped up in the snow. I went over and had a look at it, but thought it must have been left by the party with the dog."

"Did it seem placed there, as if it was to be collected later?" I asked.

"It's rather difficult to say," he replied, reflecting. "But it was the right way up and of course the snow was soft. There were also ski marks in the corrie."

"Fresh?"

"I don't know, the weather was so bad with drifting snow. Oh, I also found a piton hammer on the way down, a Stubai."

"Thanks," I said to the youth. "It was good of you to report this. I've also heard there was a group skiing up there yesterday, but we've no idea where they came from, or went."

"I'll see if I can find out," Cathel offered. "It could just help."

"I presume your chaps have had a look for the rucsack?" I asked Mick Taylor, whose RAF team were then combing this vast corrie.

"There's no sign of it so far, Hamish. I've checked."

Conditions were now too bad for the helicopter to fly, but a short time later Willie came back with the report that the five people with the dog had returned and the pack which the solitary hill walker had found didn't belong to them, and they hadn't seen it. They had seen nothing but driving snow all day.

Was this rucsack a clue, we wondered, and where the hell had it gone? If there wasn't much in it, we concluded, it could easily have been lifted up in one of those horrendous gusts and blown to dear knows where. The rain now beat on the roof of the truck like a jazz drummer. Previously, it had been drizzling with light snow up the hill, albeit horizontally most of the time.

We were just about to call operations off for the day when a call came from one of the RAF groups in Coire na Tulaich. They had found a rucsack. There was frantic radio activity to establish if it was the same rucsack which had been found by the hill walker. It wasn't and there were keys in this pack. That was something positive, which we could possibly use to identify the owner, if he was one of our missing three. Cathel had by now found out more about them. They all worked for Britoil; one was a reasonably experienced climber, another had done some hill walking, whilst the last man was a novice.

The radio messages kept coming in from the RAF hill party. They had found the rucsack about three-quarters of the way up the corrie near a gulch, and as soon as I heard this I felt that we now possibly knew where the men could be. There had been several accidents in this area in the past. Climbers coming from the summit of the mountain in bad weather have to steer on a bearing due west after a dog-leg from a subsidiary peak in order to gain safely the bealach or col at the top of the Coire na Tulaich. This, in turn, in summer and winter, offers an easy descent back to the road at the cottage of Altnafeadh. If one goes too far to the north on the initial descent to the col, a matter of a few degrees, it takes you out on to broken ground, which, when it approaches the side of Coire na Tulaich, drops steeply in nasty slabs and cliffs. In winter these are usually festooned in ice.

My thoughts took me back to another time. "Willie, remember that chap who fell up there in 1972, from the Alpine Climbing Group?"

"Aye, I do. Didn't we take the body down next morning?"

"That's right, we slid him down on the stretcher for a bit, then the chopper came in. Two of the others in his party had exposure and frostbite. They'd done Crowberry Gully." What I recollect about that call-out more than anything else was Bill Hook of the BBC who had come up by Glasgow taxi, directly from the BBC Club bar, still in evening dress. He was hoping to film the operation for a documentary which he was doing on mountain rescue. One of the team had remarked as he stepped into the slush from the cab: "Cripes, here's a member of the South Ribble Rescue Team . . ."

We were now told there was also a rope in the recovered rucsack, and it looked as if it had been recently used. Also with it were a Rollei camera, a broken crampon and a duvet jacket.

"I wonder if that crampon could mean something?" I asked Mike Hall. "Could it have been broken when the rucsack fell?"

There was a mark in the snow where the pack had slid down the slope, and some broken pieces of cheese. The top of the pack had partly ripped off in the fall.

"Well, at least we have something to go on, now," the Sergeant said. "We'll see if we can identify those keys for a start."

There was no need to give an official return-to-base call, because everyone was on the way down. Weather and darkness held the cards. Call-out for the following morning was for 8.15 a.m. There was not much point in making it earlier, for that was first light and the search now had to be concentrated in Coire na Tulaich. It wouldn't take long to get up to where the rucsack had been found. To search in the dark that night would have been pointless, as someone could easily have been caught in an avalanche and the chances of any of the men being alive was not very high. This would be the second night out in the blizzard and the conditions were so severe that it would be doubtful if even experienced mountaineers with modern bivouac gear could have survived in such an exposed place. The helicopter took off for Fort William where it would refuel and stay overnight. The RAF Rescue Team were now scheduled to stay locally and help us again in the morning. All our team headed home to lick their wounds, dry their boots and have a pint.

"I'll give SARDA a ring," I suggested to Cathel. This is the Search and Rescue Dog Association; the dogs are used for locating missing people, in both avalanches or in open country.

"Fine, Hamish, do we need reinforcements for tomorrow?"

"I don't think so, thanks. There's not enough room in the corrie for more than sixty people; we'd be standing on each other's toes, otherwise – with our crampons. But we could do with twenty bleepers for the RAF lads as they don't have any. Perhaps you could try and get them from the Lochaber team."

Willie took the truck back down the glen to charge up the radio batteries. Later that evening Mick Taylor called to see about plans for the following day and we discussed the various possibilities. Meantime, the Press hadn't been idle. They descend at the first hint of human distress with the zeal and singleness of purpose of blowflies. My 'phone and the 'phones of most of the team members rang incessantly. I knew they would be out in force the following morning. They always are if there is a hiccup in the rescue such as this one, when we take some time to locate the missing climbers.

I phoned up for a detailed forecast. There was no hope from the Met office. If anything, it was going to deteriorate.

John Grieve rang later in the evening. "I might go up with Davy Tod a bit earlier, Hamish. We want to get away from the hordes."

"That's all right, John. I'll be up there before dawn myself, but keep in touch by radio."

"Fine, I'll see you."

The weather wasn't considerate enough to improve just because we were going back up the hill. It was, as predicted, worse. The rain continued its mad dance on the roof of the rescue truck and everything looked sponge-like. Even the snow on the hills, what we could see of it, appeared like a grey marshmallow which some disgusted chef had thrown out of his kitchen.

I arrived at Altnafeadh just as the slight improvement in visibility presaged dawn. Shortly afterwards, cars, trucks and Land-Rovers began to crowd all available parking space. I climbed into the base truck with Willie and Cathel MacLeod.

"Another beautiful West Highland day," I observed, shaking the rain off my anorak hood. "The snow will be delightful."

Willie had the base radio on and there was a slight break in its usual contented hum.

"What was that?" I asked.

"Dunno," Cathel replied. "Someone must have pressed the tit of their mike, I suppose."

Outside, most of the team were making final adjustments

to their snow gaiters and rucsacks before setting off. The conversation was of the usual order.

"Hey, Walter, have you got a spare radio battery?"

"Bloody hell, which bastard's pinched my Mars bar?"

"That malt was good last night."

"Aye, but it didn't improve your darts."

"Oh, my head!"

I had waited to get the dogs up in front of the main body of searchers and Sergeant Kenny MacKenzie, an old friend, who was then the Rescue Co-ordinator for the Highland Constabulary, had come down from Inverness with his dog, Echo, as well as Jim Patterson, known as 'Scooby', from Fort William. I asked Scooby to go on ahead, and though we didn't have a spare radio for him, the other members of the team wouldn't be far behind so, if necessary, he could relay any message to them. Kenny followed later.

There is not much formality in the Glencoe team. The lads more or less decide which area they want to search and this works well, for the climbers naturally gravitate to cliffs and gullies and the shepherds and the non-technical climbers concentrate on the easier ground. Will Thomson, Paul Moores, John Hardie and Ian Nicholson all took to the Buachaille side of the corrie. Others went up in the wake of Scooby, whilst the remainder, including the RAF, spread out across the corrie floor and its westerly side.

The helicopter arrived from Fort William and attempted to fly into the corrie, but each time the pilot tried to man-oeuvre the machine into the large snow basin it was repulsed by ferocious wind and turbulence. We could see this quite clearly from the base truck. The Wessex came limping back to base and appeared to expire on the heather alongside us.

There was another spluttering over the base radio. This time it sounded as if someone was trying to get through. I looked enquiringly at Cathel and Willie.

"Hey!" I said. "Where's John Grieve? He phoned me last night to say that he was going up earlier. I wonder if he's broken down somewhere with his car and is trying to contact us?"

Cathel, with years of diligent Police observance behind him, cut in, "No, Hamish. I saw his car just up the road there. He must be up on the hill."

"That's his car all right," Jimmy Waugh, one of the local constables, confirmed. Ronnie Rodger's voice came clearly over the radio.

"Hello base, hello base. Ronnie here, do you read me? Over."

Willie grabbed the mike. "Loud and clear. Pass your message, over."

"I'm with John Grieve and Davy Tod, Willie. They have found a body."

I took the mike. "Can you give their location, Ronnie?"

"Yes, Hamish. It's just above where the RAF found the rucsack last night, to the left of the gulch going up into the corrie."

"Thanks, Ronnie. We'll have a stretcher sent up and extra help."

Some of the team who had been standing by at base for such an eventuality now set off with the stretcher. John Grieve describes what happened that morning as he entered the corrie with Davy Tod.

"Davy and I headed up the gully in deep snow. It was light by the time we reached the place where the rucsack was found. We then climbed directly out of the bed of the gulch and very soon found a wedge of cheese, probably the one the RAF found. Afterwards, we continued up the face and then bore right for a bit and walked right up to the body. He was uncovered and had head injuries. It would have been possible to have seen him from across the corrie, but not from below. I can't imagine how the RAF didn't find him the previous night, because they searched for some time after they had found the rucsack. As we couldn't get base on the radio, we started to slide the body down towards the gully."

Paul Moores, who had been going up to his search area with Will Thomson, Ian Nicholson and John Hardie, had spotted John Grieve and Davy Tod and traversed over to find out the score, but as he didn't have a radio, he couldn't inform base. He continued up on a separate line from Will and John Hardie, whilst John Grieve and Davy Tod carried on down with their cold companion until they spotted Ronnie Rodger.

Higher up Will and John Hardie stopped to put crampons on. There was a lot of nasty looking ice above, where the climber had fallen. Will was now ahead of John Hardie, with Paul Moores away over to the right. It was difficult, the ice being both soggy and dangerous and they were climbing unroped.

I decided to go up the hill now as obviously the centre of operations was going to be in Coire na Tulaich and the helicopter managed to shuttle several parties up a short way to near the entrance of the corrie. Richard Grieve and Jim Morning came with me, with a further stretcher. We made our way up the side of the gulch, on the summer path, now covered in snow and ice. The rain still lashed down with a soggy splatter into the snow cover and the wind had risen again.

John Grieve had left the body with the group who arrived in Ronnie's wake and had set off up the corrie with Davy Tod again. Mike Hall borrowed a large plastic bivvy bag from one of the RAF team and the body was put into this, then slid down into the gully. The stretcher arrived shortly afterwards and some of the team sledged the corpse down to the snowline, falling en route into deep holes where the snow spanned the thundering stream.

Seldom had we been so wet. The rain seemed to fall in continuous lumps. My plastic climbing boots were filled with water, and the wind hammered away at us like a truculent shadow-boxer. Will, who was on the snow slope above the face, down which the climber had fallen, was whipped off the ice and, like Bob Hamilton the previous day, was only saved by his ice axe. Will is a tree-feller by trade, having the strength of a Centurion tank.

He was the first to see the second body. It was face-down, lying as if he had stumbled, fallen and lain there to die. He was poorly clothed for such an environment. Paul arrived almost immediately. They saw that he had only a slight head injury, and no other apparent damage, for there was no sign of blood. But of course the wound could have happened somewhere else. Paul shouted the news down to Ian who had the only radio and was suffering from an ankle injury.

"What's that up there?" Paul pointed. "See that thing flapping about 150 feet above?"

Will looked up. "Dunno."

They both started up the slope instinctively feeling that they were about to witness another tragedy unfolding. The cloth or plastic which Paul had seen was in a cluster of snow-splattered rocks. The wind was ferocious up there and away to their right John Grieve, Davy Tod and three RAF men were heading up towards them from the col. It was a scene like Scott's last journey.

When Paul and Will approached the snowy rocks, they saw that it was the edge of a space blanket flapping. This last man was lying in a shallow scoop in the snow. They assumed that he had died from exposure. An ice axe was stuck upright in the snow a short way off, looking lonely and somehow symbolic.

We heard of this latest find over the radio a few minutes later and in the meantime John Grieve's party had reached the scene. The others, joined by Ian and John Hardie, had the two bodies dragged down on to the snow slope below by then. Will and Paul decided to rope one body directly down the face into the corrie whilst the others opted to take the remaining corpse to the col and lower it to the rescuers below.

The operation went smoothly. Will, who abseiled down an ice face to receive the body when Paul lowered it, got a shock at first. As the corpse was being lowered, its jacket got pulled off by a spike of rock and this heavy, ice-encrusted garment thudded on to the ledge beside Will, who thought for an instant that it was Paul who had fallen. We recovered the bodies at the end of the second lower and took them both down the corrie. By this time the first one had been taken right down to the snowline and out by helicopter. Bob Hamilton returned to the upper corrie with the stretcher as we had only two stretchers with us on the hill.

I contacted the helicopter on the radio to ask if he could try to come into the corrie to lift the two bodies. "We'll give it a go," the pilot said cheerfully enough.

As we struggled down the snow-filled gulch with the stretchers we saw the Wessex through the angling sleet, crazily making its way up to the entrance of the corrie. It reared and shook like a bucking broncho, then swung away, partly lifted by the wind. Presently the pilot's voice came over the RT. "Sorry, chaps, just can't make it in there. There seems to be a wall of turbulence keeping us out of that hole."

"Thanks, anyhow," I replied. "We'll take the bodies down to the snowline. It'll only take us about half an hour."

"Wilco, just give a call and we'll pick them up and any other gear."

We were sinking in the snow waist-deep in places, sometimes through to the stream below. Not that this made much difference to our general discomfort – it was impossible to be wetter.

The weight of the stretcher didn't help our plight and I watched Bob Hamilton in front. This was his second sortie down with a body. On several occasions he was only prevented from disappearing by holding on to the shafts of the stretcher as if they were parallel bars. I was reminded of another weary traveller, John Bunyan's Christian, when he got bogged down in the Slough of Despond with that invisible weight on his back. Below, the Press were assembled ghoulishly uncapping their biros. These three fatalities coming after a series of mountain accidents which had swept the Scottish Highlands over the past few weeks had caused a stir of public concern. The reason for this carnage was mainly the severe weather. We all trundled off home to take off our dripping clothes and soak in our respective baths; a few of the more dedicated, not feeling wet enough inside, returned via the Kingshouse and Clachaig bars.

We never did work out what had happened to the three unfortunate men. I talked with two chaps the following day who had met a party of three male climbers going up the access path of Buachaille Etive Mor the day before the three were reported missing. If they were the men that we found, it is possible that they took the relatively easy climb of Curved Ridge to the summit. That day the morning weather hadn't been too bad, relatively speaking, and they would only get the full blast of the storm about midday when it broke. About then, too, or shortly afterwards, they could have been heading down from the summit on the normal descent route to Coire na Tulaich. The wind must have been in excess of 100 m.p.h. that afternoon, for it was a storm which stood out in a period of savage weather. Where the one man got his slight head injury is not known. How did the crampon found in the rucsack get broken? Perhaps the man with the slight head injury had fallen and broke it, or even tripped and broke it, thereby causing the wound.

On their descent from the summit they would have been heading right into that fierce wind and blasted with lumps of stinging snow blown from the mountainside. It would have been virtually impossible to see, let alone read a map and compass accurately. They only had to be a fraction out with their bearing to steer on to the treacherous and steep ground where they were found. What happened then? Again, it can only be speculation. It was the least experienced man that was found huddled in the snow scoop and the most experienced at the bottom, the first climber located.

Could it be that he was leading the way down and disappeared over the edge, leaving his ice axe stuck there, pointing out his fate? Had then the other two just succumbed to the elements? One doesn't behave logically in such situations; exposure victims do the most irrational things. I was not surprised that the man spreadeagled on the rocks was underclad for the conditions that day on the mountain, even though a down jacket was found in one of the rucsacks. It is quite common for exposure victims even to shed protective clothing in their confusion. Did the spreadeagled man on the rock just give up and lie down to die or remain where he fell?

There is no way we will ever know the answers, but it does seem likely that they had done a climb. Two had harnesses on. The rope, which appeared to have been used, then hurriedly coiled and put in the rucsack, plus other climbing gear, pointed to them having done a route. We don't know and perhaps it doesn't really matter. Nothing will bring them back and there are no real lessons to be learned from the accident, except perhaps that they should have left a note of where they were going. Even if they had done so, we wouldn't have found them much sooner in such horrendous conditions. Buachaille Etive Mor is a big and cruel mountain.

12

ROPE COLLAR

"He was ruddy lucky!" This comment by Will Thomson was Glencoe's understatement of 1983. On 22nd February Lawrence Gornall fell 700 feet from McArtney's Gully on Gearr Aonach and lived. Fate is fickle in these matters. Another lad could slide not many feet from a snow patch in the Bidean Coire and be paralysed. But Lawrence Gornall was lucky.

That day I had been working on Stob Coire nan Lochain making a BBC dramatised documentary of a rescue described in my book, *High Drama*. At 4.20 p.m. I was on the last helicopter flight of the day. John Poland, an old colleague, was at the controls, with Joe Brown, Paul Moores and myself as passengers. In the gathering dusk as we flew down the Lost Valley, the peaks of Gearr Aonach and Beinn Fhada flanking its sides, I watched the dot-like figures of climbers heading tent- and hostel-wards after a full day on immaculate snow. From habit my eyes roamed over various routes, but a climb like McArtney's Gully isn't done very often.

I had made the first ascent myself a few years before, and had named it after Jim McArtney, one of my climbing instructors killed in a Ben Nevis avalanche. Jim had been the salt of the earth and always went out of his way to help people. I must say that it's cause for reflection when I find climbs which I did as first ascents are subsequently responsible for the death or serious injury of others following, but people die on mountains as they do elsewhere, and it is unfortunate that climbing accidents are often given banner headlines, while those least qualified to pass judgement often offer ill-informed criticism. That evening I doubt if I even spared an eye for the final steep ice-filled corner of McArtney's Gully, where it breaks on to the summit crest. If I had, I most likely would have seen Lawrence Gornall's friend Simon Fay fall some 300 feet before he was jolted to a halt by their 11-millimetre nylon climbing rope. Lawrence's belay held.

Further up the valley at 4.00 p.m. nineteen-year-old Susan Banford, the most inexperienced member of a party of eleven, had a narrow escape. She fell, or rather slid, 250 feet down ice, arrested, fortunately, by soft snow. Her arm was broken but she was mobile and her friends helped her down. They were some of the dots over which we flew, quite unaware of what was taking place below.

That morning Lawrence Gornall and Simon Fay had left the floor of the Lost Valley, just beyond the big shoulder, and took to the East Face of Gearr Aonach. It was their intention to climb Rev Ted's Gully. Unfortunately it is a sad reflection on the clarity of winter climbing guides which I and others compile that these lads entered McArtney's Gully instead of Rev Ted's which lurks in the vestry-like depths of a defile to the left.

It was beginning to get very cold in the upper part of the gully. When Simon Fay fell 300 feet, it would, in normal circumstances, have been the end of that particular attempt. But Simon proved only to be suffering from extensive bruising and, after a short confab, they decided to have another crack at it with Lawrence taking over the lead.

Lawrence climbed the first pitch, then Simon clambered up to Lawrence's now familiar stance, having fallen past it once before! He got his breath back and they changed places, Simon now belaying his friend. Lawrence moved on, climbing carefully. McArtney's Gully is harder than the Rev Ted's; it was too hard for Lawrence in the prevailing conditions, so he prudently decided to retreat, but not in such an uncontrolled fashion as Simon, or so he thought. He intended to abseil. To enable him to do this they each untied from the rope and Lawrence doubled it over a belay. In a few minutes he started to lower himself down.

Just below, in the ranks of those using the Lost Valley as a highway from the summits to the glen, were three policemen from the Liverpool area. Pausing at the Lost Valley boulder they saw the two climbers in the upper defile of McArtney's Gully. In fact, they could see Lawrence abseiling quite distinctly. But one moment he was abseiling and the next he was rapidly accelerating in a free fall towards the valley floor 800 feet below.

Though the top section of the gully is a chin-touching slope, lower down it is broken in a series of steep terraces, like the rungs of a wide ladder. In a decorative gesture, nature has placed sure-footed rowan trees in various cracks and 'plots'.

After dropping like a rag doll over the terraces, near the completion of his fall, Lawrence crashed into the sinewy arms of a rowan, broke several stout branches, and continued his journey. He came to rest on the very lip of a mini-cliff, still conscious. His helmet was shattered like an eggshell, but his head was all right. The abseil rope had coiled tightly round his neck as if on a winch capstan.

The three policemen were galvanised into action, one going down for the rescue team and the other two climbing up to where Lawrence had landed, a short way above the valley floor. They were quite convinced that he was dead, for it was impossible to appreciate that someone could have survived such a fall. Down a snow slope, yes, such accidents are fairly frequent, but not down a high-angled face festooned with boulders. They were amazed to find him alive and conscious, and quickly cut the rope from his neck.

The subsequent rescue operation worked like clockwork. I got the call from the Police before my boots were off. It was Cathel MacLeod's soft West Highland voice.

"An accident on McArtney's Gully, Hamish. It seems that

the second climber is still on the route near the top. The chap who fell came right down the face. Also, there's a girl with a broken arm at the big boulder."

"Sounds interesting. Can you get a chopper, Cathel? It's a great night with no wind."

"Right, Hamish. See you at the lay-by."

I contacted Doris to do a call-out and in minutes had parked my car opposite the Lost Valley and was heading down to the bridge over the River Coe. From here the path follows the Allt Coire Gabhail to where the stream disappears underground just at the start of the great boulderfield. The snow was crisp underfoot and the stars bore down like bright tintacks. An unusual night for a rescue, I thought, it's too good.

Willie came on the radio.

"I have the truck at the sandpit lay-by, Hamish. What gear do you need?"

"All the equipment for a big lower, Willie. One 500-foot rope, casualty bag, stretcher. Can you advise on the helicopter?"

"Cathel tells me it's due in twenty-five minutes. Also," he paused for a moment, "Ronnie Rodger has gone up after you and Mike Hall's just left with the stretcher."

"Thanks, Willie."

I had by this time reached the broad valley floor. There seemed to be a headlamp convention, lights were everywhere. A couple of chaps came to meet me.

"The girl's over here."

"Fine."

She was in good spirits but was obviously suffering from shock and cold. I asked her if she wanted a trip in the helicopter. She seemed partial to that, so I told her that it would be landing shortly. Other lights just above, on the lower slopes of Gearr Aonach, indicated the position of Lawrence and his Police escort.

Meantime there was a hive of activity at base. It was

almost a full team turnout and we also had Joe Brown and Murray Hamilton on their way up to lend a hand. Obviously there was plenty of technical know-how available for this particular incident.

I heard Ronnie's voice close by.

"What's the score, Hamish?"

"Hi, Ronnie, the girl's OK. One chap is still high up in the gully and that casualty is up there – see the lights? The chopper will be here any minute."

"What do you want me to do?"

"Better go up to the lad that's peeled, Ronnie. Ah, here's Davy, he can go up with you."

The two lights of Ronnie and Davy Gunn floated like will o' the wisps across the valley floor. Members of the team began to stream to our position and the beat of the helicopter could be heard in the still air. Soon we saw its landing lights sweep down the glen. It had made fast time. I had already alerted Willie at base to have the heavier equipment flown up as well as other team members. Mike Hall, hearing the helicopter, had rushed back up to the lay-by so that the stretcher could be taken up more quickly. Within minutes the Wessex had taken off and was fast approaching the bowels of the Lost Valley. Circling once, the pilot came on the air.

"Hello, Hamish, what do you want done first? I have some of your bods on board and a pile of equipment."

"Best if you can land and we'll take out some of the gear. Then perhaps you can fly three of the lads to the top of the face to rescue the climber still on the climb. Meantime we'll have the other chap done up ready for lifting to hospital. Then perhaps you could pick up the girl casualty here and take them both to Fort William?"

"Fine with me, coming in."

"Roger, Helicopter 34. We have a strobe marking a good landing site."

"Thanks."

Above the din of the now grounded helicopter I arranged

for Ian Nicholson, Will Thomson and Paul Moores to fly to the top of the gully and rescue Simon. The chopper took off.

In the meantime, John Grieve, Joe Brown and Murray Hamilton volunteered to climb up to Simon from the valley floor, just in case there was a hitch in landing the helicopter on the narrow crest in the dark. Paul Williams, Bob Hamilton and other rescuers went on up to Lawrence while I waited for the helicopter's return.

The Lost Valley reverberated with the roar of the Wessex's twin gas turbines as we watched it high above, silhouetted against the night sky. It seemed to take ages to inch on to the narrow ridge, but eventually they found a place and poised on part of one wheel. The three team members leapt out into the icy cold.

As soon as it landed beside us again, I climbed aboard with the stretcher. It was literally only a minute's flight to where Lawrence and his cluster of lights were perched on the edge of the cliff. I went down on the wire while the winchman followed with the stretcher.

It appeared from what Lawrence told us that both legs were broken, but it was in fact his pelvis, plus masses of cuts and bruises. We always find a fractured pelvis a difficult diagnosis to make on a dark mountainside. Once strapped securely on the stretcher, he was winched aboard. The great fan of the main rotors spilled cold air down on us and threatened to strip the windproof clothes off our backs. It was a relief when it rose and then angled down towards my strobe, still emitting its faithful flashes. A cold Susan Banford was helped aboard and the Wessex took off for Fort William.

We took off too, for base. We had just heard that Will had been lowered over 300 hundred feet to Simon and both were now at the top of the face.

"It's freezing up here." Will's voice came over the walkie-talkie. "Get a bloody move on with that chopper, MacInnes!"

"I'll see what influence I can exert," I promised him. "Meantime we're going down to the truck. It's too cold for the righteous to be out."

It was a further hour and a half before the four men were lifted off the summit ridge of Gearr Aonach. As the boys hadn't expected to be stationary for so long, they were now frozen to the marrow. On their own they could easily have come down, but Simon was suffering from exposure and could possibly have come to grief on the precipitous descent. Furthermore, they had a mound of rescue gear and ropes with them.

Lawrence's parents called in to see me after they had visited him in the Belford Hospital, Fort William. As they were leaving, his mother asked me if I knew how he got the weals on his neck. I was able to enlighten her.

A couple of days later when we were back working on the documentary in the Lost Valley, Ian and Will found the tree which had fielded Lawrence. It grew just above the clifftop where he had stopped. As Will said, "He was ruddy lucky."

13

REV TED'S AND THE OLD MAN

I have generally found that priests of the Roman Catholic faith are more cheerful than their Anglican counterparts. But 'Rev Ted' of the Church of England was the exception that proves the rule.

This stolid representative of the cloth, together with a shapely German nursing sister called Karen, were the only members of my winter climbing course in the first week of February 1966. Karen, agile, nubile and with the sleekness of a cat, was in striking contrast to the Reverend who moved with the deliberation of a bulldozer which was partly attributable to the weight of his snack box. This generous receptacle was daily replenished with goodies such as chicken legs and pâté de foie gras.

My proposal to try a new route one day met with his blessing and a *"bitte schön"* from the fräulein. Thus, the Rev Ted's Gully on Gearr Aonach was ascended for the first time and duly christened.

At a later date I climbed its two other branches, for it forms a trident near the top. In recent years we have had various rescues from these reaches of Rev Ted's, close to the heavens. One, a dramatic helicopter winching operation, used the full extent of the 300-hundred-foot winch wire to extricate a girl with a broken leg from the original finish, the Left Fork. The incident I wish to describe now occurred in the Central Fork, the hardest of the three.

James Thomas, a scientific officer, aged fifty-six, was climbing solo – always a serious undertaking and sometimes a one-way ticket to disaster, especially in winter when snow conditions are variable or avalanche-prone. 19th February

1984 was a black Sunday. That day four climbers were to die on Scottish mountains.

Rev Ted's is possibly one of the most popular of the standard snow climbs in the region and that Sunday several parties were front pointing their way up; that is to say they were deploying the modern ice-climbing technique of kicking in the front points of their crampons and holding on to the ice with two drop-pick ice axes, their droopy snouts biting like anchors into the surface.

James Thomas was on the crux of the Central Branch when he fell. He should have dropped 700 feet as Lawrence Gornall did next door when he took off from McArtney's Gully, but the gods smiled on James and he providentially landed on a ledge some sixty feet below, sustaining a broken ankle and bruising. It was also an act of Providence that two able American climbers were at grips with Rev Ted's Left Fork when they heard his cries. Within ten minutes they had reached him and after shouting to other climbers on the valley floor to get help, they set about the task of lowering him.

I didn't have to be a prophet to know that there would be trouble that Sunday. Over 150 vehicles were squashed within the confines of the glen lay-bys and many were mini-buses, each capable of carrying sixteen people. By the law of averages, something was bound to happen.

It was 2.00 p.m. when Walter Elliot 'phoned.

"It's started, Hamish, an accident on Rev Ted's, broken ankle. I think some lads are trying to lower him down."

"Did his mate come down, Walter?"

"No, another chap ran down from Coire Gabhail." Walter and Willie rarely stoop to call it the Lost Valley.

"Right, Walter, I'll give the fuzz a buzz and get the old egg-beater over from Leuchars. Can you ask Doris to do a call-out? The piper's lay-by, Walter. The sandpit will be too congested. We can't land the chopper there, anyhow."

"Aye, OK."

As I put the 'phone down, I thought, Walter is never flustered. Even in the most traumatic crisis he appears to take an academic interest as if considering the form of the Scottish rugby team.

Though I was first up at the rendezvous point with our Land-Rover, I decided not to go up to the climb. I had been astounded by the sheer volume of parked cars. Every lay-by was overflowing and some vehicles were even parked on the main road. I had spoken with Cathel MacLeod before leaving and a helicopter was on its way. Ronnie Rodger was the next to arrive. I suggested that he took off right away with his radio and advise on the situation. I knew there would be plenty of team members available to follow him.

Though we didn't know it at the time, a Rescue 34 Wessex helicopter was already on Ben Nevis. Al Coy, the pilot, navigator John O'Neil and winchman Mick Anderson had come on shift at 1.00 p.m. They made up a formidable rescue combination with vast experience and Mick is a keen mountaineer into the bargain. They had been scrambled for an accident in Glover's Chimney at 2.05 p.m. With them were a pair of cadet pilots who went along to see how helicopters flew in conditions where they weren't supposed to.

They had arrived in Fort William and unloaded the two cadets in exchange for some of the Lochaber team whom they then dropped off close to where the climber had fallen. This man had also been climbing solo but wasn't as lucky as James Thomas.

When Al got the radio call that they were needed in Glencoe, they left the Lochaber team attending their casualty and came south, pausing only to reload their brace of cadets. I gave Al a run-down of our situation as soon as he reached the foot of the glen. He suggested flying directly in to see if he could pick up the injured man. Mick knew the route, of course, but first they had to unload the cadet cargo.

By this time Ronnie had climbed more than halfway up Rev Ted's and was met by a fusillade of ice, knocked down by the two Americans out of sight above.

"Hey, what the hell are you doing?" he yelled.

"Sorry," one of the Americans shouted, "but we've got to lower this injured guy."

Ronnie apologised when he got up to them as he thought it was climbers fooling about. The two Americans had done a good job and James Thomas was being slid down the icy surface with the minimum of discomfort. I told Ronnie that the chopper was on its way, so they halted the lower and waited. Other members of the team were only a short way below. John Grieve arrived with Paul Williams and Bob Hamilton pounded up with stretcher and casualty bag.

As the helicopter nudged within spitting distance of the face, one of the Americans asked, "Is it all right if we finish the climb now? You seem to have plenty of muscle power."

"Sure, lads, thanks," Ronnie replied. "Have a good climb."

Something was wrong in the helicopter. The team watched as it hovered 200 feet above. Mick was hauling on the winch hook and navigator John O'Neill was thumping the drive unit with his gloved hand. Al came over the team walkie-talkies.

"Sorry, boys. The winch is jammed. It'll go down but not up. We'll have to come down to base and see if we can fix it."

"Right, Al," I replied. "I'll advise the hill party. They may not have got that due to the engine noise."

The Wessex landed cheek by jowl with a cluster of cars and, with the engine still running, John climbed up to the gearbox housing beneath the main rotor. I was surprised to see him, as he put it, "gently belt the winch hydraulic selector valve with the butt of my Very pistol". It is consoling to know that such a primitive act can cure a technical misdemeanour. Apparently all was now well with the winch for he turned towards the rescue truck, beamed and gave the thumbs-up sign as he climbed back into the cockpit.

Meanwhile, back in Rev Ted's, the boys weren't idle. James had been put on the stretcher and was being lowered on a 500-foot rope down hard snow. When the helicopter returned, they stopped operations and he was winched aboard. After picking up the two cadets from base, Al flew directly to Fort William and James was transferred to a waiting ambulance which took him to Belford Hospital.

In Glencoe, rescue operations were temporarily run down and the lads made their way back to base. But not the helicopter crew. The two cadets were put out yet again (could they have been beginning to feel unwanted?), for the Wessex now had to go back up to the north-east face of Ben Nevis. The Glover's Chimney victim was dead. The Lochaber team had taken down the body to a better place for winching, and had radioed to say that they were ready for the pick-up. But by the time the Wessex arrived the weather had deteriorated and the helicopter was buffeted by high winds and nasty turbulence. It took Al with his vast know-how two attempts to enter Coire na Ciste, which in laymen's terms meant that flying conditions were ghastly.

After flying the body and some of the Lochaber team back to Fort William, they took aboard their two 'in-out' passengers again and flew to their refuelling dump at nearby Corpach at the head of Loch Linnhe. Already that day in the Cairngorms a man had died after falling 500 feet, and on Ben More at Crianlarich another climber had fallen to his death.

I returned home before all the lads came down from Rev Ted's as I had some urgent work to attend to. I kept on my boots which in the event saved both time and trouble.

It was PC Stuart Obree who rang. "More trouble, Hamish."

"Where is it this time, Stuart?" I asked with resignation.

"On the backside of the Aonach Eagach, Hamish. I have the map-reference." He gave me this and continued, "I looked it up, it's on the North Face of Am Bodach. A girl called Georgina Brockley was with a party from the Holiday Fellowship. They were all standing on the top and suddenly she was gone. Apparently she fell down a snow gully and disappeared."

"I'll go back up the road to the truck, Stuart. Can you contact Fort William to see if they can intercept the chopper before it goes back to its nest?"

"I'll see what I can do, Hamish."

Am Bodach is the principal peak at the easterly end of the Aonach Eagach Ridge. As I drove up the glen, I reached for my walkie-talkie and tried to contact Willie at the truck. Some of the lads still descending from Rev Ted's answered.

By the time I drew into the lay-by, word had spread among the team that another accident had occurred and they were standing by at the truck. The map-reference proved to be a point to the north and east of Am Bodach, and didn't tie in with where a body would land when falling from the summit. We decided, as it was getting late, and as the helicopter winch was still temperamental, that one of the team should go with a radio and check the map-reference. Will agreed to do this and was off in a couple of minutes, followed soon by Bob Hamilton with a torch as it was getting dark. The rest of us awaited the helicopter. It flew low up the glen. There was something purposeful about the way that Al handled that large machine just above the valley floor. Mick's voice crackled over the speaker near the ceiling of our truck.

"What's the score, Hamish?"

"A girl's fallen on the other side of the ridge. Could be pretty bad, for it's hellishly steep ground. How many can you carry?" By this time he had almost reached us.

"We're full up with fuel; only two, I'm afraid."

"Right. John Grieve and I will come up."

"Roger."

There was no formality of doing a circle before coming in

to land. The Wessex came in like a fixed-wing aircraft and was on the deck quicker than you could blink with the rotors spinning close above the parked cars.

The now familiar cadets emerged from the belly of the chopper and, heads low, ran towards the truck. They were hailed by Willie as old friends as they had already spent hours chatting with him from the previous sortie.

As the 'in-out' cadets ran clear, John and I sprinted to the chopper. We were airborne in a couple of minutes and, donning a headset, I spoke on the intercom to Al and the crew.

"Best way in, Al," I said, "is over the summit if the wind's OK for that approach. She's fallen directly off the top and down the other side. There's a gully of sorts there and," I added, "not much to stop her before the floor of the corrie – about 800 feet below."

"I think we'll make it." His voice sounded distorted on the intercom. When I adjusted the helmet so that it fitted more snugly round my ears I could hear him loud and clear.

Flying conditions were bad now. A strong south-easterly wind was speeding across the mountains and dropping down into corries on the lee slopes. The result – vicious down-draughts.

We crested the ridge of Am Bodach after a long spiral ascent to gain altitude. It was like leaving a harbour, the shelter of the glen, for a wild, wide, invisible sea. Al took the helicopter in a once-over-look-see of the summit, then dipped down into the northern corrie.

Will and Bob Hamilton had now been contacted, but they kept going, for there could be complications in finding the casualty, as well as the temperamental winch problem.

The large sliding door of the helicopter was open and we scanned the glinting snow for any unusual colour or blood trail. I spotted her. She was with two men, members of her party who had managed to climb down by an easier route.

"Below, Al. Two o'clock, on the snowfield."

"I see them."

The machine wheeled round and fluttered down into the depths of the corrie.

Mick fired a smoke-flare from the Very pistol through the open door as a wind indicator. There was no place for Al to land close to the casualty, so he put down about 200 feet beneath the party. Mick, John and I jumped out on to iron-hard snow and, carefully avoiding the rotor blades on the uphill side of the aircraft, we climbed to that desolate-looking group. We had a stretcher with us as well as first-aid.

Mick and I examined her while John took off her crampons. She was critically injured, but still alive. We put the stretcher alongside and gently lifted her on to it in the same position in which she lay, careful not to flex her back, for we suspected a spinal injury. Her head wounds were ghastly and there was blood everywhere.

I cupped my hands alongside Mick's helmeted head and shouted, "Where's the oxygen kept, Mick?"

He yelled back its location in the aircraft and I gave a thumbs-up sign. I glanced up the North Face of Am Bodach as Mick contacted Al on his personal remote talkback radio. I could see blood streaks a long way up the slope. She must have fallen at least 700 feet. Mick turned to John and me and motioned us to go down to the helicopter which was still marking time on its slippery slope-hold. There was too much noise for conversation. Her two companions came down with us. I indicated, by sign language, for them to keep their heads low – if they wanted to keep them.

We barely had time to get strapped in before the aircraft rose and started to sidle up the slope. It climbed higher as it approached Mick and the casualty. John O'Neill, who had come down from the cockpit, stood by the winch control as the hook descended.

For the next minute or so I was busy getting the oxygen resuscitator organised and didn't realise that Mick was clipped on to the wire with the stretcher, but the winch refused to budge. Al had to take off with Mick and the casualty still on the end of the wire and flew to a slightly easier snow slope some way down the mountainside. Here, descending slowly, and with the help of John O'Neill as a 'height guide', he lowered Mick and the girl on to the snow. Mick managed to keep his footing and hold on to the stretcher on the icy surface. The starboard wheel on the uphill side of the Wessex was almost nudging the snow. I glanced out and saw the top of Mick's helmet just level with the helicopter floor. It was obvious what John Grieve and I had to do – we leapt out when we got the OK from Al, fortunately remembering to unplug my headset!

Getting the stretcher aboard was awkward even though we are used to standing on steep snow, and the forty-knot ice-cold draught chucked down by the rotors took our breath away. With amazing skill, Al kept the big machine on an even keel, while continuously being buffeted by the wind. There wasn't much clearance between the main rotor and the uphill slope either.

Once Georgina Brockley was safe inside, we helped each other up over the sill, the last man being left little dignity as he was hauled up by those inside. The door slammed shut and we were off. Al knew the urgency of the situation, for Mick had told him of the girl's condition. The Wessex swooped down the corrie flat out, just above snow level, almost touching the intervening ridges. As I cleared vomit from her mouth, I could feel the wind hitting the fuselage of the chopper causing it to yaw and dip. As her pulse was so weak we gave her cardiac massage; in fact it was almost undetectable, especially with the vibration in the aircraft being driven to its limits.

Now the oxygen mask was on and we could pause for a moment. My clothes, face and hands were splattered with her blood. I had plugged in the headset jack again and could speak with the crew. "She's in a bad way, Mick, I doubt if she'll pull through."

Mick, who had been monitoring her pulse, looked up and shook his head. "I think she's probably had it."

Al now took the helicopter up the edge of Loch Linnhe and in a few minutes he was putting it down in the car park at Fort William alongside the waiting ambulance. Georgina was put on the ambulance's oxygen supply and speeded off to the Belford Hospital. There she was registered as 'dead on arrival'.

Al spoke to me when the ambulance had left. "You know, Hamish, I feel a bit bad about this business. If I hadn't gone to refuel, we may have got to her sooner and saved her life."

"That's nonsense, Al," I retorted. "Nobody could have done more; we don't deal with crystal balls." There really was nothing more we could have done for Georgina. But I knew how he felt. Often in retrospect you think of ways in which you may have been more efficient on a particular incident; how you could perhaps have adopted a course of action which may have helped to save a life. In this particular case, had Al not refuelled the aircraft, another scramble could have occurred where a full load of fuel aboard could have been vital.

After filling up again at Corpach, Al and his crew set off for their base at Leuchars, picking up their cadets for the fourth time back at Glencoe base at the piper's lay-by.

Later that evening a party was reported missing overdue in the Mamores, the mountain range between Ben Nevis and Glencoe.

Also that day a solitary skier had parked his van some distance from the White Corries chairlift in Glencoe, intending to go ski mountaineering. He was a married man from Fort William, with two children. In Glencoe we slept peacefully enough that night, unaware that he was lying on the glassy slopes of Meall a' Bhuiridh.

14

THE LONELY SKIER

I was having an early night and in bed about the time Christine Gibson telephoned the Fort William Police Station. She was concerned that her husband, forty-four-year-old Wallace, had not returned from a ski-mountaineering trip on Meall a' Bhuiridh in Glencoe.

Initially, Christine was not unduly worried, for Wallace, as well as being an experienced ski mountaineer, was a very capable climber and had regularly set off on solo expeditions with skis and skins into the Scottish mountains.

PC Stuart Obree was still on duty in Glencoe that evening. It was to continue to be a busy shift for him. Fort William contacted him to check out the chairlift car park and establish if Wallace's van was parked there. Wallace was the Hoover/Hotpoint service engineer for the area. Earlier he had been employed as an engineer with Rolls-Royce and before that was manager of Nevisport in Fort William, a climbing-cum-ski store, which reflected his involvement with mountains.

Stuart drove up Glencoe in the Police Range Rover and turned off at the western edge of the Moor of Rannoch, taking the narrow road leading to the White Corries chairlift. It was dark, of course, but still not difficult to establish that there were no vehicles in the car park or immediate area. He reported back to Fort William by radio. Then he made a tour of the hostelries in the area, just in case Wallace had been tempted by an all-night party, not an infrequent event in the Scottish Highlands, but still no sign of the van. In case Wallace had changed his mind and gone to Aviemore (the other ski complex within striking distance of Fort

William), the car parks there were also given the once-over by the Police, again negative.

On the Monday morning all the team members were back at their daily toil: John and Richard Grieve were diving for scallops, as was John Hardie; Bob Hamilton was fishing for prawns with his creels; Peter Weir, Davy Gunn and Will Thomson were felling trees; Denis Barclay was installing a transformer for a new power line; John Anderson, Davy Tod and Ronnie Rodger stooped over their lathes and machinery at the British Alcan Works in Kinlochleven and Fort William, while Peter Harrop, a recent recruit to the team, dismantled a gearbox on one of the upper tows on Meall a'Bhuiridh. Mike Hall, who has a similar job to Wallace Gibson's with Servis, was operating locally that Monday, while Alan Thomson, a freelance writer, had driven down to Glasgow, had heard on the BBC News in the Glasgow branch of Nevisport that Wallace was missing and drove straight back to Glencoe. Paul Williams, a pressure-chamber expert at the Lochaber Underwater Centre, had motored to work in Fort William. Paul Moores, our high-altitude team member, was running an Army mountaineer-ing course based at their outdoor centre in Ballachulish. Ian Nicholson, usually a super-active team member, had con-tracted an arthritic virus and climbed painfully out of bed while Hugh McNicol, who owns an ice-axe factory, reported to his polishing wheels that morning for he had more than one axe to grind. Kenny MacKenzie joined his wife Marie for another day behind the counter of their local restaurant. He had hung up his Police Sergeant's mountain rescue co-ordinator's cap and had taken to catering for the other basic needs of tourists. But he's still Honorary Secretary of the Search and Rescue Dog Association, and takes out his own dog, Echo. That leaves the brothers Walter and Willie Elliot; both involved with their respective flocks until the call-out.

This was the roll-call for this particular incident and in

attendance, representing law and order, were PC Cathel MacLeod and PC Stuart Obree. As for me, I had gone round to Kinlochleven, our other ugly-sister local town at the head of Loch Leven, to have my car serviced. It was here that Alex Gillespie 'phoned me.

"Hello, Hamish, Alex here. I'm 'phoning from the Police Station in Fort William."

I was surprised that he had managed to track me down to this garage. Alex is a photographer based in Lochaber who had been a director of Nevisport and is also a member of the Lochaber Mountain Rescue Team.

"What can I do for you, Alex?"

"A friend of mine is missing, Hamish, one of our local Fort William climbers, Wallace Gibson, you know him?" Alex put me in the picture. "I've just been speaking with Chief Superintendent MacInnes here. They found his van on the old road, down from the chairlift car park. Stuart Obree didn't see it last night as it was more or less hidden, way off the road on a track. Jimmy Bannerman spotted it at first light." He continued, "Can you call out the team?"

"I'll do that right away, Alex."

He added, "We've just come off an abortive call-out in the Mamores so a few of the Lochaber lads are here, all kitted out; will we come down?"

"Fine, I'll see you at the car park in about half an hour."

I contacted Willie Elliot and jumped into my partly serviced car, praying that the wheel nuts had been tightened as I headed back along the sinuous road to Glencoe. Willie Elliot had assiduously worked his dialling finger through the call-out list. It isn't always easy to contact the lads during working hours, but those alerted put down their tools, switched off their compressors, tied up their boats, left stock-taking and put the collies in the barn. Ronnie Rodger stopped his lathe at the British Alcan factory in Fort William, jumped into his car and was about to set off for Glencoe when he saw a familiar sight – the two 'in-and-out' cadets being taken on board the Wessex in the Fort William car park. Ronnie drew alongside. Al Coy and his crew had already been out at first light in the Mamores before the missing party had turned up unharmed. Flying conditions hadn't improved overnight and a southerly wind was gusting at forty knots with bad turbulence.

"You'd be as quick motoring to the ski tow, Ronnie," Mick Anderson, the winchman, shouted to him above the din. "We'll have to refuel, just done an hour's flying in the Mamores."

"Aye, no sweat, Mick," Ronnie replied in his usual cheerful manner. "I'll push on in that case."

I called in at home to pick up my rescue gear and gave Cathel MacLeod a ring. "Has Fort William told you about the call-out for the missing skier, Cathel?"

"No, Hamish, but I knew Jimmy Bannerman had found his van."

"Well, we're heading up now and the Wessex is coming from the Fort. We've done a call-out."

"Good, I'll be up in a few minutes."

I was first at the ski-tow car park with the Land-Rover; Willie had arranged to take up our truck. Paul Moores arrived five minutes later. Paul, a top-line instructor and British Mountain Guide, has vast experience as a mountaineer and was just then planning an expedition to Lhotse Shar. He had come up in an Army Land-Rover.

"Hi, Hamish, what's the score?"

I told him what I knew.

"I know Wallace; he's not a bad climber."

Just then we heard the helicopter droning up the glen by Buachaille Etive Mor. It came slowly towards us, obviously heavy with fuel and passengers, and put down on the tarmac forty feet away. The door was already open and I saw the familiar figure of Mick Anderson. Beside him were Alex Gillespie and Donald Watt, the Lochaber team leader.

As there were only about four or five men immediately

available to search, I suggested that we deploy the chopper
for a quick once-over of the mountain to allow more time for
the lads to assemble.

"Where to, Hamish?"

"How about along the summit ridge, Al? Then a sweep of
the two corries, Cam Glen towards the main road and the
easterly glen, Coire an Easain?"

"Fine."

Lay people put the helicopter on a par with the kestrel or
peregrine as a search instrument. In fact, they are always
helpful, but to varying degrees. If the missing person can
wave something or is dressed in a colour that shows up, then
a helicopter can be invaluable, especially as so much terri-
tory can be covered. But immediately you get a comatose
casualty, or one whose clothing blends with the surroundings, you have to be very sharp-eyed to spot him. There is
also the monotony of the search; quartering a hillside in a
seemingly endless series of elongated zigzags hour after hour
can tire the keenest eye. A few years ago pigeons were
trained in America to react to yellow, the common colour
of life rafts. These birds were enclosed in a perspex dome
on the belly of the helicopter and they recorded 'sightings'
by a peck on a signal plate, which, as well as informing the
crew of the bird's find, also ensured they received an auto-
matically dispensed reward of grain. I thought about these
pigeons as we studied the many avalanche tips which extended
from the upper slopes of the mountains to the floors of the
corries.

We were also looking for ski tracks, but the snow was icy,
apart from drifts, and these were hard to see from the air.
Alex spotted a couple of climbers in a gulch in Cam Glen.
He took the helicopter down close to them, but they
obviously had nothing to tell us and were practising ice
climbing on a short glassy pitch.

After about forty minutes, Al said, "If we're going to take
the mountain rescue lads to their respective search areas,

Hamish, we'll have to go back. I'll have to refuel at Corpach in about twenty minutes."

"OK, Al."

As we came down on the car park, I saw that quite a few of the team had gathered round the truck. They were obviously ready to go. We had the search areas allocated in five minutes and the first flight was off.

The Meall a'Bhuiridh massif is shaped like a plum pudding or a maiden in dire need of an 'F-Plan' diet. There is a summit ridge running to the south-west, forming a T with another ridge which connects Clach Leathad (pronounced Clachlet) on the south and Sron na Creise on the north. In the oxters of the T thus formed lie Cam Glen on the north and Coire an Easain to the south. Both are mighty corries, popular with red deer when the autumn amour takes their fancy. In fact Meall a'Bhuiridh means Peak of the Rutting.

Meall a'Bhuiridh was the first mountain in Britain to be developed with a chairlift for skiers and it provides good but often icy conditions for that dedicated, tough, wind-resistant, individual, the Scottish skier.

After we discussed the possible route that Wallace could have taken, I asked the Lochaber boys to search the area of the Flypaper, a very steep ski run, and then continue up over the summit of Meall a'Bhuiridh to drop into the head of Coire an Easain. Donald Watt, Alex Gillespie and Kenny MacKenzie were in this group, Kenny with his avalanche dog. It seemed likely that Wallace could have attempted to gain the summit by the ridge just east of the Flypaper as, in the past, he had skied the summit ridge to the T junction and skied on to the summit of Clach Leathad. Some more of the Fort William team were to be dropped off on the ridge close to Clach Leathad itself. Ronnie Rodger went with Lochaber team lads, Andy Nicol, Terry Confield and Willie Anderson.

We thought that Wallace's Ford Escort van being so far from the car park might be explained by the fact that the old military road continues up round the edge of the Moor of Rannoch to a height of over 2000 feet. This provides a natural means of access to the east side of the mountain which leads higher up to the corner of the Flypaper.

The White Corries staff had been questioned without success to discover if Wallace had been seen the previous day. There was one report of a skier being seen heading for the top tow, which seemed to fit Wallace's description. Denis Barclay decided to investigate this further.

As the helicopter was shuttling search parties to their locations, others used the chairlift to gain the Plateau below the main ski complex. I had decided to stay at base to co-ordinate the search, for help was streaming in from other Lochaber personnel as well as from casual climbers. The Glencoe team were concentrating mainly on the Cam Glen area, although I didn't think this a particularly high priority area, as a ski mountaineer is very mobile and capable of covering great distances.

Wallace could be miles away. However, we were well aware of the danger this valley presented to those who strayed off the piste. There are various runs on the mountain, the names of which were created by the fertile imaginations of the Glaswegians who were the ski pioneers of this area. Runs which denote the joys or hazards ahead, such as Mugs' Alley, the aforementioned Flypaper, the Haggis Trap and Happy Valley. Etive Glades is the run closest to the edge of Cam Glen, the slope of which ices up regularly in winter. Being both steep and well peppered with rocks, it has claimed the lives of several unsuspecting victims.

While I was with Al in the helicopter, Paul Moores, John Hardie and David Cooper, owner of a local craft shop, had gone up the chairlift. From the top of the first lift they cut to the right, across the Plateau, which is a wide shelf about a third of the way up the mountain. When they descended into Cam Glen, Paul suggested that David should head upwards, following the valley, while John and he climbed the face of Sron na Creise above them.

"We'll meet you either at the head of the glen or back at base," Paul said. "John and I will work along the summit crest to the T junction with Meall a'Bhuiridh."

"Fine, see you later," David said as he set off.

Back at base, I was monitoring the various groups when we got a call from Denis. Denis, Walter Elliot and John Anderson had traversed the 'fall-line' of earlier victims of the Cam Glen. John knew the area well because, like Denis before him, he had worked for the chairlift company. They had come across the two climbers whom Alex had spotted from the helicopter. It turned out that the day before they had met a solitary skier who was planning to go up the summit of Meall a'Bhuiridh, then descend to the east to an abandoned house called Ba Cottage.

"Hello, base, Denis here. Can you advise on the colour of Wallace's skis, please? We may have a clue from a couple of lads here who spoke with a solo skier yesterday. He had blue skis."

"Stand by, Denis," I said, "I'll ask Cathel to contact Wallace's wife."

"Aye, thanks, Hamish. This gives a new slant, so we'll head towards the summit."

"OK, Denis, I'll keep you posted."

It transpired that Wallace didn't have blue skis, so this lead, like so many on any given search, came to nothing. But it illustrates the useful co-operation that exists between a rescue team and the Police when they pool their joint resources.

Alan Thomson, after he heard the news about Wallace being overdue, had returned to Glencoe from Glasgow. When he arrived at base, I suggested that he search the north side of Sron na Creise, beyond where Paul and John had ascended.

"Mike Hall's over there, Alan, you'll contact him on channel 2."

On the morning search with the helicopter I had spotted

a large avalanche on the east side of Meall a'Bhuiridh. This had been reported again by Donald Watt's party. I asked Ronnie Rodger and Andy Nicol, who had already checked their search area, to investigate it. They were flown there with probes and shovels.

The two cadet pilots, after emerging from the yellow belly of the Wessex that morning, were still keeping us company at base. Here, at the White Corries car park, things weren't so boring for them as at yesterday's location down the glen. As we watched, immaculate zip-suited dolly birds were heading for the piste, unaware that they wouldn't look quite so polished après the traverse of the muddy path across the Plateau. There is a peaty expanse of half a mile between the top of the first chairlift and the ski slopes, which in times of thaw resembles soggy Black Forest gâteau.

I asked Willie to take the Land-Rover down to the Glen Etive turn-off so that he could get better reception than from the car park with those in the Cam Glen. Cam Glen valley is over the high shoulder of Creag Dhu, the long buttress wall of the Plateau.

About this time, John Grieve and Hugh McNicol arrived. They had been at work or uncontactable earlier – or both. Eric Moss had also joined us and, as always when Eric is about, we were bombarded by tales of his Army service with some fascinating insights on his term of imprisonment in a Japanese concentration camp. A story which I particularly like is the one where he smuggled an office typewriter past his regimental guardroom secreted under his kilt. Eric is no longer active on the hill, but busies himself at the truck, doubling 'mess' duties (making soup) with the duty of quartermaster (looking after rescue gear).

As it hadn't snowed overnight, we were fairly convinced that Wallace wouldn't be covered over by snow, unless in an avalanche, but I was growing concerned as we still hadn't any positive leads. He seemed to have vanished without trace. The Wessex was now being deployed to drop people

off in new search blocks and bring others back to base. My
map was a mass of lines and boxes showing the areas which
had been gone over, some twice. Cathel came into the truck
from the Police Range Rover to say the rescue control at
Pitreavie had called, asking if we required another helicopter. A Sea King from RAF Lossiemouth was available.

"Yes, please, Cathel," I said. "Al's winch is still buggered
and we may have to pull someone out of a difficult hole yet."

Just as the next radio call came in, the rather ungainly
shape of the Sea King rose into view over Kingshouse
Hotel.

"Hello, base, Paul Moores here. We've found the skier.
Over."

Reception at the truck was poor, but Willie, who was
acting as relay at the Glen Etive road end, came on.

"Did you get that message, Hamish? Paul and John
Hardie have located the missing skier."

"Yes, thanks, Willie, we got that – just. Can you ask Paul
for more details when he's got time?"

"Aye, OK."

Paul and John had, as intended, climbed the face of Sron
na Creise and then made their way searching along the
summit ridge towards the T junction. David Cooper by this
time had gained the head of the glen and slanted left up
towards the summit of Meall a'Bhuiridh. When Paul Moores
and John Hardie were traversing the ridge, they could see
the rest of the team below in Cam Glen and also observed
that a section of the head wall had been omitted in the
sweep. They made a mental note to check this area on the
way back to base.

It was almost 4.00 p.m. as they cut across, below the level
of the ridge, to gain a natural line across the head of the
glen. This would take them back on to the ski slopes above
the Plateau, then down to the car park. They didn't see any
ski marks here, but Walter Elliot and John Anderson had
found indistinct traces further across this traverse. All Paul

and John saw was a broken ski ahead, and, below that, a line of blood. They quickly cramponed down the steep slope and followed the grisly trail, knowing full well what they would find at the end of it. Initially, they saw no sign of Wallace, due to the convex slope.

Suddenly they came to him and, as they had expected, he was dead, his clothing blending perfectly with the boulders. They found his rucsack a short way below and contacted us by walkie-talkie on the spot. Wallace had fallen about 500 feet down hard snow and ice. He had obviously died instantly. There was no clue, however, as to the cause of his fall, for he was an experienced skier and the traverse line which he was following is not difficult. Possibly it was one of those terrible gusts of wind that made Al's flying so hairy on the previous day, throwing him off-balance.

Not only had we failed to find Wallace with the helicopter that morning, having flown directly above him at least twice, but Walter, John Anderson and Denis had been quite close and David Cooper must have passed a few feet from his body. This illustrates how difficult it is to locate an unconscious person or a body, especially if their clothing is of a colour similar to the surroundings. Had we deployed a rescue dog here there would have been a definite possibility that he would have been located quickly.

I gave out a general call, and once we got a fix on their location over their fading radios, we relayed this to all parties on the hill and to Al who headed into Cam Glen with his Wessex and soon spotted Paul and John holding a fluorescent wind marker. The ground was both steep and icy. Because the winch was still out of action, Al attempted to put a wheel on the slope, but it just wasn't possible. There was not enough clearance for the main rotor and furthermore a vicious wind was charging down from the col above in dangerous gusts, threatening the aircraft. He gave maximum torque and pulled out.

He gave us this news over the RT. He was also running

short of fuel. But the Sea King from Lossiemouth had now arrived and the pilot agreed to take over from Al. The Sea King always appears to be more ponderous and deliberate than the Wessex. It is of course a bigger machine with a range of 930 kilometres (577 miles) and can carry, in addition to the four-man crew, up to seventeen passengers. It also has an automatic hover capability, which is used mainly over water, and full night-flying equipment. It seemed to be making heavy weather of getting into upper Cam Glen, which just then bore a striking resemblance to a wind tunnel.

As soon as the Sea King pilot spotted Paul's party (more of the lads had arrived by now), Al descended to the car park. The two cadets didn't seem disappointed at the prospect of going home at last, and the liferafts and other equipment necessary for sea rescue were put back on board. I thanked Al, John and Mick for their help. It had been quite a scramble.

I did a general recall, but diverted those in the vicinity of upper Cam Glen to go to the accident location in case assistance was required. The Sea King pilot lowered his winchman almost 250 feet on to the inhospitable ice slope beside our team. He was fielded by a couple of the lads and the wire was taken back in again as the big machine wheeled round, harassed by a whiplash wind. The winchman was not happy. Only experienced climbers would feel at home in such a place, but the lads kept a watchful eye on him. The Sea King came in again, this time with the stretcher ready on the winch-wire hook.

The pilot started to lower it in a buffeting wind, then decided that conditions were just too bad. Had Wallace been alive it would have been another matter, but it wasn't worth the risk in order to evacuate a corpse. He knew that we could get him out with our own stretcher.

The helicopter was being shunted about and the stretcher was wound back in again on the wire. The pilot took the aircraft in a wide circle and came back, this time to recover his winchman. Things were getting hairy. The wire snaked out again, swinging like a pendulum. The heavy hook and swivel were almost down at the group level, just out of reach, and as lethal as a mace. A gust hit the chopper and the pilot had to take evasive action by losing altitude and side-slipping down the corrie. He knew that there was a strong possibility that the winch-wire hook would catch on the rocks and cause a crash, so he took the decision to cut the wire. This can be done by triggering a small explosive charge guillotine. The wire fell well clear of the party and the chopper came back to base. The pilot and crew were shaken by the incident and took some time to recover. The hapless winchman didn't of course have crampons or an ice axe, but John Hardie and some of the Lochaber boys guided him to a safer stance.

I spoke with the pilot and soon realised that it wouldn't be possible for him to take any of us up into Cam Glen. Indeed, it had been unfair of me to ask after his harrowing experience. So I told one of the lads to dash up to the chairlift and ask Philip Rankin, the manager, to hold things – I knew that they were due to go off home any minute.

We then hurriedly got together a party from the Lochaber chaps and our own team and, taking a stretcher with us, we set off for the chairlift in the gathering dusk.

Before I left, I told Willie Elliot that we would make the evacuation right down the long Cam Glen which runs towards the Glen Etive road end, but as the River Etive successfully prevents access to the road, we would have to head for a point some two miles further down where it might be possible to ford.

From the top of the chairlift we cut diagonally across the Plateau to the lip of the Cam Glen. To say that we set a brisk pace would be an understatement, but we did pause at the icy slopes dipping into the glen to put on our crampons. This only took a minute and we were soon spiking across the icy slopes towards the distant dots which we knew to be the rescue party. Peter Harrop, carrying one half of the stretcher, was just behind, determined, I think, not to be left trailing on this his place of work. I was in front with John Grieve and called to him, "That must be John Hardie up there, cutting steps for the winchman." I pointed with my ice axe. Two figures were just visible between opposing walls of rock. I had been wondering how John Hardie would get on with this ascent, as he didn't have a rope for the winchman. But John had spent years on the Scottish mountains and had for a time worked as one of my climbing instructors. RAF property was in able hands.

We heard the helicopter once again. It flew back up the glen but instead of progressing to the violent upper regions, veered left to the edge of the valley towards the spot where John Hardie and the winchman had emerged on easier-angled terrain. With a lot of trouble, the pilot managed to get the wheels more or less down on a snow ledge. John and the rescued rescuer jumped aboard, helped up by another crew member – it's quite a high jump to get into that aircraft, even on easy ground. In so doing, John accidentally dropped his radio and it is a compliment to the Japanese manufacturer that when I found it after being interned in snow for several months it functioned perfectly.

Meanwhile we put Wallace's body on the stretcher and started to sledge him down that long trough of snow and boulders which constitutes the floor of Cam Glen. I ran ahead, picking the best line connecting the snowfields and avoiding boulders. I literally had to run, for there is always an element of healthy competition between Lochaber and Glencoe teams, each trying to outdo the other; on this occasion it was a mad race.

Meanwhile, Willie Elliot and the others were not idle. Ronnie Rodger, Mike Hall and some Lochaber team members set up a rope traverse across the River Etive, for the boulders and banks were coated in ice. They also had the generator and floodlights working.

Here, there was some comic relief. Most of us were wearing crampons, except the Clachaig barman, Doug Gordon. After emulating John Grieve, who had leapt on to a boulder in midstream, Doug discovered that it was coated in ice. His feet just didn't want to know this landing place and shot off; he broke the surface of the icy water with his behind, this followed by complete immersion! After the team's happy reaction to this unsolicited baptism, the stretcher was clipped on to the aerial ropeway and hauled over the river in a comparatively sedate fashion. More prudent members of the team also utilised this means of gaining the other riverbank.

With the end of the rescue, harsh reality set in once again. Most of our team had at least known Wallace, but to some of the Lochaber boys, Alex Gillespie in particular, he was a personal friend. It is always sad when the cold fingers of fate rest on a colleague. We didn't say much that night, but quietly went our respective ways.

15

THE DEADMAN BREAKS A LEG

'Land of the Mountain and the Flood'; Sir Walter Scott's description of the Scottish Highlands certainly applied in January 1984. The new year arrived in a wave of torrential rainstorms which blocked roads and caused landslides, filling the pubs with climbers, who had nothing to do. Apart from a few fleeting breaks in the weather, the winter was literally a washout as far as mountaineering was concerned.

On Wednesday, 21st March, Liverpudlian Chris Snellock and Robert Wilson from Sheffield arrived in the glen. They had intended to come up the day before, but Chris was delayed with work. Their tent was pitched on the banks of the River Coe, close to the Clachaig Inn. Surprisingly, it didn't freeze that night and was in fact quite mild. In the morning, after cooking breakfast over their Gaz stove, they packed their climbing gear and headed towards the West Face of Aonach Dubh.

In recent years, Scottish winter climbing has taken off in the popularity polls, and in the depths of winter mountaineers arrive from all over the world to participate in this sometimes masochistic pastime, where, often as not, one flails crutch-deep through soggy snow while being buffeted by storm-force winds. In such conditions natural belays get obliterated by the heavy snow cover and climbers resort to deadmen belays. Winter mountaineering certainly exerts a strange and fascinating spell. Possibly because when you do get a good day, there's nothing like it in the world. All that snow gives it a fairyland quality, like being in a white paradise, albeit somewhat chilly!

Unfortunately, there was nothing mystic about that day

Chris and Robert struggled up to the Screen. The Screen is a drainage line off the face from Middle Ledge which solidifies in winter to give a steep ice climb. Only now water was running over the ice but they did manage to get up No 3 Gully, and afterwards the Smear, which, like the Screen, is a frozen candelabra of ice in winter.

The next day the weather didn't improve and Chris and Robert joined the rank of climbers forced to sit in their tents all day and read. On the Saturday they went up to Aonach Dubh again, this time to the far end of the West Face, where it forms one of the entrance walls to Coire nam Beith. No 6 Gully was their objective.

That morning as I drove up through Glencoe, I thought that I'd better tell Willie Elliot to put up avalanche warning posters. I could tell that the snow was in critical condition after heavy falls and, from the look of the clouds, more snow was threatening. Without thinking, my eyes roved over the many climbs visible from the A82. I noted several parties were already on the hill and saw two figures at the base of No 6 Gully. These could possibly have been Chris and Robert.

Chris now takes up the story.

"At the bottom of the climb we came across another couple of climbers who thought that the snow in the gully was too wet. Robert and I had earlier discussed the possibility of avalanches, but we hadn't seen sign of any, despite the heavy falls of the previous day. It had been snowing steadily above 1000 feet. We decided, wrongly it turned out, that conditions were safe and opted for No 6 Gully."

No 6 Gully is a Grade IV climb and one of the winter classics of Glencoe. The route is over 800 feet in length and in a hard winter provides an almost continuous runnel of ice, a veritable Cresta run with 70-degree sections.

Chris continued: "We decided to lead alternate pitches, Rob taking the first and the crux pitches. When we were on the crux pitch it started to snow again, but as we were engrossed in the climbing, we didn't think much about this at

the time. The ice tended to be quite good, a bit on the soft
side perhaps with the mild weather, but this made the placement of our ice axes easier and they held well. One of the
troubles, however, was that the fresh snow smothered the
ice and the belays; this probably held us up.

"We unroped when it appeared to be little more than a
plod. By this time we were well up the mountain at a point
where the gully blends into the upper slopes, beyond where
the Upper Ledge cuts across. I carried the rope over my
shoulder in case we needed it again. There were about thirty
centimetres of new snow on top of the old and, realising that
it could be unsafe, we prudently kept to the side of the gully
where there was less chance of the surface layer breaking
away.

"Up until now I had been ahead of Rob, breaking the
trail, but I had rigid crampons on and they kept balling up
with snow. This made things harder and more dangerous.
Rob took over the lead as his crampons seemed OK. We
kept to the right, then followed a bend tending right. Then it
was straight up, followed by a leftwards slant.

"I suppose we had been going for about eight to ten
minutes from where we had unroped when it happened.
Visibility was poor as we had climbed into snow clouds.
Suddenly Rob, who was some thirty feet ahead, cried out. A
crack had appeared about ten feet in front of him and
simultaneously the whole slope started to move downwards
with cracks opening in front of me like breaking china. I
tried to ram in the shaft of one of my two ice axes but my
feet were swept from under me and I was engulfed in a sea of
snow. Initially I was convinced that either I would stop
myself with my ice axe or that the snow would stop. But
neither happened. I gathered speed, pushed by a tremendous and unrelenting force, first right, then left. At one time
I think I was hurtling down head first on my stomach, but it
happened so fast that I can't be sure. I lost my ice axe (the
other one was in my harness holster) and in desperation

attempted to stop myself by digging in my fingers. All I could think of was my family and my girlfriend. I thought that I could see my whole life flash by, but of course that couldn't really have been the case. Somehow or other I managed to turn myself over, or it may just have been the flow of the avalanche, but I found myself in a sitting position. I could only see around me a uniform whiteness of swirling snow. I thought, If I survive this lot I'll give up climbing, and as I took off over the big pitch all I could feel was a weightlessness followed by a bone-racking thud as I landed on my rear.

"I must have gone over at least another pitch before the snow stopped. It only paused for a fraction of a second, but it was long enough for me to feel the power of the snow freezing and tightening all around me, and to realise that I couldn't breathe, and would never be able to dig myself out. Suddenly I shot forward again over another pitch, then started to slow down. I began to do a breaststroke and when the avalanche finally stopped I was miraculously on the surface.

"I felt disorientated and had difficulty focusing. I realised that Rob was quite close by, with only his head and arm showing. He was moaning, obviously in great pain. I stumbled over the snow boulders of the avalanche tip and started to dig him out. Pausing for an instant, I took my whistle from my pack. Somehow or other the rucsack had remained on my back. I put the whistle in Rob's mouth and told him to blow it six times, once every two seconds [the standard distress call]. He managed it once, then was silent. I had to keep telling him to blow as I excavated the now solid snow around him.

"I was worried that I had bashed my head in the fall and asked Rob to check my eyes to see if the pupils were the same size. I could feel grit in my mouth, and when I spat out I could see blood on the snow. I later discovered that I had bitten my tongue.

"Then I heard shouts from the path across the valley,

beyond the stream. Two climbers were calling, asking if we were all right. I shouted back that my friend was injured, with a broken leg as far as I could ascertain. But they couldn't hear and after a short time came across. As they climbed up the avalanche tip towards us one of them picked up our rope, which had been carried past where Rob and I came to rest. They also found my ice axe."

These two Glaswegian climbers, from the Rannoch Club, had themselves been avalanched and buried at the head of the valley. With amazing luck they had dug themselves out, one suffering from an injured leg, and while beating a thankful retreat towards civilisation they saw both No 5 and No 6 Gullies avalanche one after the other. A short time later they heard the distress whistle.

Chris again: "The climber with the injured leg stayed with us whilst his friend ran down for help. We tried to protect Rob from the cold, but he's big and we couldn't move him because of the intense pain. Stupidly I tried to undo his crampons to free his legs rather than cut the straps and of course hurt him even more than necessary. We kept ourselves occupied by excavating a platform for the stretcher to rest on when it arrived. It was gruelling work, for by this time the snow was set like plaster of Paris.

"To take Rob's mind off his injuries we told him jokes. Normally he's a quiet individual but if he laughed his leg hurt even more, so instead we just took turns at holding him while the other dug the platform. It must have been about half past three when the accident occurred. By this time it had stopped snowing."

My trip through the glen that morning had taken me over to Tyndrum, a nondescript scattering of houses which boasts two railway stations, Tyndrum Upper and Tyndrum Lower. It was to the lower of the two that I literally pushed my way through snowdrifts to meet a passenger. It's the sort of shelterless station where a commuter might perish with exposure in winter. I was back home and had just come in from salvaging a snowballed pet sheep when Willie Elliot 'phoned.

"There's a chap from the Rannoch Club just come in, Hamish." And he relayed the situation in No 6 Gully. Willie did the call-out and I tried to telephone the local Police Station to arrange for a helicopter, but there was no one there. So I rang Fort William, the Divisional Headquarters, where I spoke to Chief Superintendent MacInnes (a namesake, but no relation). I asked him to try to get a helicopter as soon as possible and gave him the map-reference of No 6 Gully.

"Can you contact me at the Elliots' house? You've got the number."

"Right, Hamish, I'll try and fix it for you."

On helicopter flight duty at Leuchars that day were Flight Lieutenant Steve Murkin, navigator John O'Neill and winchman Bob Danes. At 1615 hours they were scrambled for No 6 Gully, Aonach Dubh, Glencoe. Within minutes they had clipped on their safety harnesses in the yellow Wessex of Rescue 34. The rotors began to turn.

I arrived to find Walter and Willie waiting for me outside their cottage. I had first-aid and Walter took a folding traction splint. Willie was to operate base.

"I wonder if a chopper will get across today, Walter?"

By now we were traversing the steep slopes on the Aonach Dubh side of the stream.

"I have my doubts, Hamish. This pea soup is gae low." In fact we could see that the cloud was on a level halfway up No 6 Gully.

In about thirty-five minutes we began to climb up towards the base of the gully. The snow was slushy and ahead of us we could see the avalanche debris from No 5 Gully. The avalanche had come right over the Icicle, which is the first pitch in the gully in winter. In fact the Icicle hadn't formed properly and wasn't connected with the base of the cliff as it often is at this time of year.

On cresting a small gulch I saw two figures ahead, then a third, partly hidden in the snow of the avalanche tip which had come out of No 6 Gully. I gave a shout and one of them waved his ice axe. It was obvious to us as soon as we got close that conditions were still highly dangerous. For all we knew it could still be snowing above. This I thought was likely and a further avalanche was possible.

"You'd better switch on your avalanche bleeper, Walter. I don't like the look of this place. It could be a quick burial for us if it avalanches again, especially when the chopper comes in."

There had been a couple of incidents in recent years where soundwaves from the rescue helicopters could possibly have triggered avalanches.

"I don't have mine with me," Walter replied, grinning.

"Well," I returned, "you've managed without it for twenty-five years. Let's hope your luck won't run out now."

We had almost reached the dejected-looking party.

"How is he?" I enquired.

"I think he's broken his thigh," someone said.

I examined the casualty and found that he was in fact suffering from a broken leg and probably other injuries. It was impossible to say, since he was still angled into the hole which his friend had enlarged. I told his pal, Chris, to take the rope which was lying on the snow boulders, and tie one end round a tree to one side of the avalanche and about forty feet above, so that we could secure his friend. The survivor of the separate avalanche gave Walter and me a hand to partially extricate Rob, so that we could put the splint on.

Willie came on the radio asking if anything else was required. On the way up he had kept me informed and told me that the stretcher and casualty bag were on the way. He now said, "A radio call has come through from the Fort William Police and the ETA for the helicopter is in approximately twenty minutes."

"Fine, Willie, that was fast."

Constable Stuart Obree was now at base, in constant touch with Fort William Police Station via the Range Rover radio.

Rob seemed to be having spasms of pain every minute or so. I gave him Fortral orally as I had no more powerful painkiller with me. Predictably, this didn't have much effect. I contacted Stuart at base and asked him to telephone our local GP Dr MacLeod to check if it was permissible to increase the dosage. It was, but it was very apparent a few minutes later that it didn't help Rob much.

John Grieve arrived. Behind him, further down the slope, were Davy Gunn, Peter Weir and Ronnie Rodger. Peter had one half of the stretcher. Bob Hamilton was dogging his heels with the other half. Bob told me later that on a previous rescue Peter had beat him up the hill to a casualty and this time he was determined to get ahead of Peter, even if he had started five minutes behind.

Paul Williams appeared; behind him Mike Hall. I was surprised to see Mike, thinking he was still on holiday on the Costa del Sol. It turned out that he had been, less than twenty-four hours before, and was now feeling the damp Scottish cold seeping through his tan.

"Anybody who doesn't have their avalanche bleeper with them had better go over by the tree belay over there," I called. I was surprised to see that everyone went over except John Grieve.

"Don't tell me you're the only bugger with a bleeper other than myself?"

"No, I forgot mine too," he burst out laughing.

Some wag shouted over that this could be the rescue of the Lost Leader.

"All I can say to you, Grieve," I muttered as we assembled the stretcher, "is don't ever pick on me for not taking my hard hat on the hill again." I dislike wearing a crash helmet.

Mike Hall shouted over, "I can hear the chopper."

A few minutes later Willie came on the radio. "What's the plan, Hamish? The helicopter has just come in."

"We'll be ready in a couple of minutes, Willie. We're just about to put the casualty on the stretcher."

Walter and some of the other lads joined John and myself in lifting Rob out of the hole, splinting him properly, and getting him on the stretcher. He was heavy, and it obviously hurt, but it had to be done. The helicopter came down to one side of us and the pilot was sizing up the situation. I spoke to him on the radio.

"Can you give us a few more minutes?" I asked.

"Sure, just give a call and we'll come in."

They beat time above the stream, slightly higher than our position. I was still worried about the avalanche risk. In fact it had started to snow and had obviously been doing so above off and on for many hours.

Chris Snellock came over to me. For the first time I noticed that he had a limp.

"Is it all right if I go down now, Hamish? I'm feeling rather cold, and my leg hurts."

"Sure, will you manage OK?"

"Oh yes, just a bit slow."

"Good, we'll get your pal off to hospital fairly quickly now. I suppose the other chap who gave you a hand will come down with us."

Once Rob was secure the others went back on to safer ground with the exception of John Grieve and myself who stayed with the casualty.

"Tell him to come in, Ronnie," I shouted over. "We're ready."

The records from Rescue 34 describe the conditions: "Weather a problem, with bad turbulence and occasional snow showers. Wind south-easterly gusting to forty knots."

That doesn't sound too bad to someone not used to working with helicopters in the mountains. However, if you add to it a cliff rising sheer in front of the machine for over 800 feet, the confined space of the narrow valley, a cloud ceiling nudging down on to the rotor blades and nowhere to put down in an emergency, you will realise that there are better places to fly!

Things didn't go with the usual precision on this winching operation. It was my fault. With great difficulty the helicopter got positioned about seventy feet above us, rearing and yawing. The winchman descended on the wire, his yellow helmet appearing like a halo in the diffused light. We had considerable problems fielding him, for the avalanche tip was steep. However, we managed to grab him at the third swing and kept a tight grip of his harness until he unclipped from the winch wire.

The noise of the helicopter was deafening and flint-like fragments of snow stung our faces and eyes with the downwash. I have mentioned that Rob, the casualty, is a weighty lad and I made the mistake of placing him too far up the stretcher. The result was, when the helicopter started to winch him up together with the winchman, he tipped down so that his head was lower than his feet and it looked like he could have slid out of the securing straps. Although there was no danger, it seemed precarious and the winchman was obviously worried. I signalled for him to come down again, but due to the turbulence the pilot could not lower the stretcher back on to the mini-ledge which had been cut by the avalanche survivors. The winchman had to touch down on the high-angled jumble of snow boulders. We then had a hell of a job holding the winchman in position together with the stretcher while I disconnected the clip to re-sling the lift wires on the stretcher. I lost all feeling in my hands as I had to take my gloves off for the re-rigging operation. At last this was done and both patient and winchman swung out and up free from the slope. Three minutes later, with considerable difficulty due to wind and turbulence, they were hauled inside.

I breathed a sigh of relief and turned to John.

"I thought for a moment that we were going to break our long-standing record of never losing a patient in an evacuation!"

Robert Wilson made a complete recovery and within a few months was back climbing again to quite a high standard. As well as breaking both ankles he had also broken his femur and by the nature of this injury surgeons thought it was probably done by the deadman belay plate which Robert had attached to his harness when he fell. Chris, too, despite his 'falling resolutions' was back on the hills again, none the worse for his ascent and descent of No 6 Gully, Aonach Dubh.

"Right!" someone shouted. "A free pint. Let's go!"

At base the rest of the team were standing by. Some were drinking Guinness, others lemonade. Denis had his pipe kindled and the density of the ensuing fug in the rescue truck rivalled that of the cloud above.

"It looked a tricky bit of flying, that," Cathel MacLeod commented as I took a swig of Irn Bru.

"It was, Cathel, but for once I don't know if it wouldn't have been safer in the chopper. Things were a bit dodgy up there today. I've got a sixth sense for avalanches after having been caught in so many. I didn't like it one bit."

"Hey, Hamish, telephone." It was Walter shouting from the doorway of the Elliots' cottage.

"Oh, no," I moaned, "I bet it's the Press."

But it wasn't. A rescue team's work is never done. Where we were off to next is described in the final chapter.

16

OFF THE PISTE

"Telephone, Hamish."

Kicking the snow off my boots at the front door, I went in and picked up the receiver in the hall. I could see into the living room where, as usual, an enthusiastic fire was blazing. Beside it was a wet, steaming, tired-looking climber with a cup of tea in his hand. On the floor beneath him there was a pool of water. It is common for avalanche victims to have their clothes stuffed with snow, including their underclothes, and this poor chap at the Elliots' was no exception. His 'padding' was now returning to a liquid state and dripping to the floor with the kind ministrations of the fire and Doris's hot tea. Though I hadn't seen him until now, I realised that this was one of the two Glasgow boys who had survived the first avalanche accident that day, and after digging themselves out of their own potential grave had answered Rob and Chris's distress whistles, one coming down to raise the alarm.

It was Philip Rankin on the 'phone, the manager of White Corries chairlift.

"Hello, Hamish, sorry to bother you. I gather you're just back from a rescue."

"That's right, Philip. I presume you have some more problems for us?"

"Correct, we have a couple overdue from the hill. They were last seen about 3.30 p.m. and the weather's pretty frightful up there at the moment. I have the ski rescue squad doing a check of the huts."

"Hold it a minute, Philip." I went outside and yelled to the lads not to bugger off pubwards as more work was in the offing. I then went back to the telephone. "Right, Philip. I was just postponing the lads' sampling of free ale. We'll be up in about twenty minutes."

"Good, Hamish, I'll be here."

We were not enthusiastic about the prospect of a search – it can be soul-destroying. You have to keep alert for hours on end, studying with diligence every unusual shape as if it was the rent collector. Furthermore, the weather was beginning to sock in and we all knew that the barren windswept slopes of Meall a'Bhuiridh are not the most conducive of places to spend a Saturday night, particularly if you'd just been debating the various well-earned merits of the Clachaig Inn, the Ballachulish Ferry Bar and another local hostelry known as the Grotto.

As a matter of fact, this whole story started with bad weather. An old Creagh Dhu Club friend of mine, Bob Clyde, who is the general manager of the Cairngorm Chairlift Company at Aviemore, had advised all potential clients who wished to ski to head for Glencoe as blizzard conditions had closed all lifts and tows in the Cairngorm area. Three people at least took this advice: nineteen-year-old Fiona MacPherson, her boyfriend, twenty-one-year-old Guy Beswick, and an American doctor friend Sheila Martin. Fiona was then an art student and Guy a textiles manager. They passed through Glencoe in Guy's BMW as Robert Wilson and Chris Snellock were front pointing up the steep clear ice of No 6 Gully on the West Face of Aonach Dubh.

As it takes a couple of hours to drive from Aviemore to Glencoe, it was after 1.00 p.m. by the time they parked their car and walked up to the bottom chairlift station. After buying their tickets, the three took the lift up the steep initial section to arrive at the edge of the Plateau. The weather in Glencoe, though not as bad as in Aviemore, wasn't exactly three star, and they had to walk across an icy expanse to gain the various other lifts and tows. Here, on the final slope, they took a further chairlift called the Cliffhanger, aptly named because, after a few hundred feet, it ends on top of a stunted rock face.

Visibility was poor. In fact, coming across the Plateau they couldn't see the upper slopes of the mountain at all, and an icy wind was blowing. But they enjoyed themselves despite everything. Dr Martin had opted to go down and wait at the car park and perhaps go for a low-level walk if she felt so inclined. Fiona describes that afternoon:

"At about 4.00 p.m. Guy and I decided to have our last run of the day as the tows stopped at 4.30 p.m. We were back up top again and as we looked for the run which we had been using, visibility worsened. Also it started to snow. We went from side to side looking for the piste but just couldn't find it. In ten minutes we were lost, lost in a white-out. We could hear neither voices, skiers or the tow. The eerie silence was frightening.

"We decided that the only thing to do was to ski downhill and to get off the mountain before darkness fell. In fact we had become totally disorientated and skied in completely the wrong direction. The angle got steep and dangerous as we went down amongst rocky outcrops.

"After about an hour our hopes were dashed, as we found ourselves at the edge of a precipice and were unable to ski further. There was a steep narrow gully leading downwards, but we were afraid that this might lead us into a blocked-off glen with no way out.

"We shouted for help, without success. Somehow, we felt that our only option was to climb upwards in the hope of finding a piste on the other side of the mountain. Taking off our skis we started to ascend with the skis strapped together in one hand and the sticks in the other, helping us to maintain balance. By this time the wind had risen appreciably and visibility was in the region of two metres, which meant that we had to stay close together."

By this time, too, down at the car park, Dr Sheila Martin was getting worried. She had watched the weekend skiers, happy and flushed with exercise, returning down the chairlift until it closed for the day, but there was still no sign of her two friends. In the meantime, some of the chairlift staff noticed the car and wondered who it belonged to. Sheila Martin spoke to Philip Rankin, who rang Glencoe Police Station and then the Elliots'.

Meanwhile, Fiona and Guy were in a white-out and worried.

"We were on steep snow when Guy dropped his skis and they slid down the mountain, fortunately stopping on the edge of an overhang. He climbed down and managed to retrieve them by using a ski pole in reverse so that the wrist loop went over the tips. He then climbed back up to me. So many times we thought that we had reached the top of the mountain, only to find ourselves on yet another ledge.

"After we had climbed for about three-quarters of an hour the wind became so strong and cold that Guy decided we would have to build an igloo for protection for the night. It was now after 6.00 p.m. We knew we would have to do this immediately before the wind got any stronger and the temperature dropped even further and darkness fell. I had now come to accept the fact that we were well and truly lost, but, strange to say, I didn't really feel frightened.

"We searched for a suitable rock in the lee of the wind to build snow walls against, for we realised that we couldn't build a proper igloo, as the snow was too powdery to form a roof. Using a ski, Guy dug down through the soft snow to hard-packed névé below. With blocks of this he built the buttress walls of the shelter while I did the pointing, cramming soft snow as a draught-excluder into the gaps.

"We built a wall about a metre high in the form of a semi-circle with the rock as the back wall. We moved inside and kept our spirits up by referring to the back door of our 'igloo' and what we would have for dinner – if we were somewhere where we could order it. We also commiserated with each other that we had left the Polo mints back in the car.

"It was bearable for about quarter of an hour or so; a tremendous relief to be protected from the wind, but then the cold started to seep into our bones. It became intense.

"Now I became very frightened and almost lost hope. Again and again we shouted, 'Help, help!' but our voices were snatched away by the wind. We thought that we could hear dogs barking, but we eventually realised that it was just the howling of the wind."

Before Philip 'phoned me he had got things going in his own backyard. The ski rescue squad had, as usual, done the check of the various pistes prior to closing down. He had then asked them to go up again and do a further check of all the huts and the various tows when he heard that two people were overdue. The squad were on the hill when we arrived, and he agreed to keep the chairlift running for us.

Philip had also found out that Mrs Jerry Thompson from Tighnabruach, whose husband, a GP, sometimes does a duty day when skiing, had spoken with the couple. She told them to ski Mugs' Alley as it was a safer run in the prevailing conditions.

I asked Cathel MacLeod, who had just arrived, if he could contact Hamish Menzies, the head gamekeeper at Forest Lodge, the Fleming estate across the Moor of Rannoch, and ask him if he could make his way up the old road as far as Ba Cottage. It was just possible that, had the two skiers succeeded in getting off the mountain, this could have been a likely line of retreat from the bad weather coming from the south-west. As Guy and Fiona didn't know the area, the idea of emerging on to the fastness of the Moor of Rannoch on a winter's night could be confusing in the extreme.

"He'll meet up with some of our lads, with any luck, Cathel."

I think we all realised that there was little hope of finding the two skiers that night. Once a benighted party goes to ground and huddles in their snow hole or shelter, with anorak hood tightly drawn, there is slim chance of our getting in touch. There was a typical example about fifteen years previously at the top of this chairlift. A young man returned across the Plateau, just about ski closing time and as the mist came down. Unfortunately, he was indoctrinated with the snow-hole syndrome which afflicts those who take survival courses. The result is that they seize any opportunity to test their knowledge in the field, often unnecessarily and regardless of the trouble it may cause to subsequent search parties. This chap made himself a home right next to the ski lift. On this particular night, the weather, despite some intermittent low cloud, had been reasonably fine and I had asked for a helicopter from RAF Leuchars. As this was searching the snow slopes using its landing light, Denis Barclay almost fell into the missing man's snow hole. Denis told him in a forthright manner: "All you had to do was to stick your bloody head out of your snow hole, Jimmy, and you could have seen the lights of Kingshouse Hotel below . . ."

However, it always makes the search easier when the lost souls are still alive, no matter how well ensconced they are in their temporary lodgings. Looking for bodies, or a comatose climber, is a different kettle of fish. We didn't know if we would be finding Fiona and Guy dead or alive. Even the most innocent slope can be lethal in winter, provided it is covered in hard snow or ice, and if there are protruding rocks below to break your fall, or perhaps your neck. That day Meall a' Bhuiridh had all three, with a blizzard thrown in for good measure – the basic ingredients for disaster.

Cathel MacLeod came over from the Range Rover. "No luck with the chopper, Hamish. The pilot had to go back to the Fort, visibility is just too bad."

"Thanks, Cathel, it was worth a try."

I asked Paul Williams and Dougie Gordon, the Clachaig barman, to skirt the east side of the mountain and have a quick check of Coire an Easain. Meanwhile Ronnie Rodger would take the old road round to the ruined Ba Cottage and keep a night eye open for the keeper, Hamish Menzies. In the gathering gloom the rest of us went up on the chairlift. It was weird, giving one a feeling of disembodiment, with just the swish of the rotating pylon pulleys and the soughing of the wind.

To the right I could barely discern the dark outline of the start of the Creagh Dhu cliffs, which run along the north edge of the Plateau. In the first steep gully, which cleaves this face, Walter Elliot and his dog Spot found a dead skier back in 1969. It had been a night just like this when we started looking for him and I had some Czech rescue service colleagues staying with me. For them it was a busman's holiday. Walter and Denis, as well as Eric Moss and some other team members, got lost that night, and Denis, who at that time had been working with the chairlift company for several years, had gone too far to the left with Walter when coming off the Plateau, resulting in their arriving on the brink of the Creagh Dhu cliff. This is exactly what the unfortunate skier had done earlier that day, only he hadn't angled off to the east to gain the top of the chairlift, but had continued down, carrying his skis and digging his heels into the hard surface of the gully. It was the next morning that Walter's collie had found him.

Now at the top of the lift we waited for everyone to assemble, then set off, following the overhead wire of the cableway which is used for carrying equipment, not people, across the Plateau. That wire nine feet above was the limit of visibility.

It is interesting to reflect on the staffing of the chairlift. The ski industry in Scotland grew up round a dedicated band of hard climbers and skiers who used to travel by hired bus from Glasgow to the middle of the Moor of Rannoch. Then, in virtually any weather and always in the dark, they walked, carrying skis and Bergens (framed rucsacks) across the peat 'trenches' of the Moor to Ba Cottage, which was then roofed and cosy, but abandoned. Using the cottage as a base, they skied mainly in Corrie Ba, a smooth sculptured cirque to the east of Clach Leathad. These pioneers were members of the Lomond Mountaineering Club and when the chairlift company was formed, they were the weekend labour.

It was some of these ex-mountaineer Glasgow hard men who had given the hill the twice-over that night and, as we approached, two of them waded out of the deep snow to greet us outside the tearoom near the bottom of the Cliffhanger chairlift. They had checked all the huts and runs as well as the Cliffhanger, but there was nothing, only drifting snow and at the top a raging blizzard. There were five in the patrol: Jack Williamson, Jack Low, Andy Pryde, Davy Hutcheson and Archie Scott. I asked where Bert Dobbie was and they told me he had retired.

"What do you want us to do now, Hamish?" Jack asked.

"Well," I replied, "we're very democratic in our pack. I'll tell you what we should do, and you pick what you want to do. We'll have to check the Plateau to the east to arrive at the old military road, then back to the car park, with a further group cutting to the north partway along. That leaves us," I continued, brushing the snow off my cap, "about enough bods to go west across the Plateau and descend partway into Cam Glen and return, checking the bottom of the Creagh Dhu cliffs on the way back."

The ski patrol opted for this.

"Have you got crampons?" I asked.

"No, but we'll be OK," one of them replied. "We've got our poles."

I hesitated for an instant, knowing that it could be an icy drop down the shoulder leading to the base of the cliffs, but I also knew they were a highly competent bunch and that they wouldn't do anything silly.

My slight misgivings proved correct, for due to the atrocious visibility they went down the face before reaching the end and found themselves kicking their heels into the icy surface of a gully. But, unlike the poor chap that Spot had found, they were prudent enough to climb back up to the edge of the Plateau and thereafter find an easier, more devious, descent line. Due to this error, though, they were late in returning to the car park, but we had given them one of our rescue radios, and Willie Elliot at base was kept informed of their various movements.

Peter Weir, Davy Gunn, John Grieve, Mike Hall and I set off in the opposite direction to the ski patrol across the Plateau. We had to travel on a compass bearing. We simply couldn't see, let alone search. To have found anyone in such conditions would have meant literally tripping over them. As I kept one eye on Mike Hall's torch ahead of me and the other eye on my compass I said to myself, one must try.

When we judged that we were about halfway across our section of the Plateau, John Grieve, Peter and I veered northwards walking abreast, about eighty feet apart, searching, as we descended towards the military road. When we came out of the cloud and snow we could see lights strung out below. Alan Thomson, John Hardie, Hugh McNicol and other members of the team were combing the lower slopes of the mountain.

Will Thomson and Peter Harrop had gone up on the chairlift after us and had headed towards the upper part of the Cam Glen. When they got there the conditions were so severe that they turned tail and headed back down. It was impossible to search. We had no contact with them as both their radios were on the blink.

We got back to the truck at 9.00 p.m. We were soaked and ice was still melting on our parkas. Willie Elliot, the Police and Eric Moss were in residence.

"Any word of the ski patrol, Willie?" I asked, kicking the soft snow off my gaiters with the edge of the truck's steps.

"Aye, we were in touch for a bit," Willie admitted, "but not a word for over an hour."

"Let's try them again," I suggested and took up the base radio mike. On the third try I got a response, but not very distinct, saying that they were now at the far end of the Creagh Dhu face and were heading our way. They expected to be back at base in an hour.

Ronnie had made contact with Hamish Menzies in the Forest Lodge four-wheel-drive Toyota. They had met up near Ba Cottage and Ronnie was heading back along the old road. By this time, Will Thomson and Peter Harrop had returned, so all the team was accounted for. Will and Peter reiterated what we already knew, that the avalanche risk was acute; the mountain was in an angry mood.

I asked Eric Moss if he would hold on until the ski patrol got off the hill and telephone me if there were any further complications.

"OK, Hamish, I'll do that."

Willie asked, "What time tomorrow?"

"7.30 a.m. up here, OK?" I suggested.

"Fine," he returned. "I'll 'phone the remainder of the team when I get back home."

"Thanks, Willie."

"By the way," Cathel called as he headed towards the Range Rover, "don't forget, folks, the clocks change tonight."

As Will Thomson was taking the Land-Rover back, I went down in the Police Range Rover. The truck would stay at the car park as a base for Eric and the returning ski patrol. In any case, it was required here at first light. Going down in the Police vehicle with Dr Sheila Martin, who was going to spend the night at the Glencoe Hotel, I asked her about her friends, Fiona and Guy, and discovered that they were not very experienced skiers, certainly not ski mountaineers, and that Fiona was wearing a pink ski suit and Guy blue. This was important for a daylight search as one can 'tune' the eyes to be more responsive to a preprogrammed colour.

There was still a lot to do that evening and I arranged search areas for the next day. I had asked Cathel to call in the RAF Leuchars Mountain Rescue Team, as well as Search and Rescue dogs via Kenny MacKenzie, who would know which handlers were available. He rang to say that Scooby Patterson from Fort William, Jimmy Simpson from Aviemore and his fellow Police dog handler, Brian Gallacher, from Inverness would be there at first light. Kenny, of course, had his own rescue dog, Echo.

I made a quick calculation as to how many searchers would be available and discovered that we could count on a total of seventy, including fifteen from Lochaber and the six ski patrol. The RAF also promised a Wessex at 0800 hours from Leuchars.

Fiona and Guy found that night the longest in their lives:

"We endeavoured to maintain our body heat, but we were shaking and trembling throughout the night. Then we tried to keep the circulation going by doing hand and foot exercises, but as soon as we stopped, the penetrating cold returned. We knew that we dare not fall asleep because, if we had, our body temperatures would have dropped and we wouldn't regain consciousness. We kept talking to prevent falling into that fateful final slumber, calling each other by name . . . 'Fiona' . . . 'Guy'.

"Five times during the night Guy cleared the suffocating snow from over and around us. It had been falling and drifting continuously, and three times we heard the rumbling of avalanches. The darkness seemed interminable and with no sign of help our spirits sank. We prayed.

"We thought of the folks at home and told each other what to say to family and friends should only one of us survive. I almost laughed when Guy said that our chums at The Fox and Hounds in Bramhope would never believe our tale, and we thought how embarrassing it would be if the story ever leaked to our local Wharfedale paper."

As a rescue team, we had discussed between ourselves the

possibility of Fiona and Guy surviving the night. It had been terrible, with high wind and very heavy snowfall. Also, we felt there was a definite possibility that they had been engulfed in an avalanche, in which case we knew it could be months before they would be found. But one must always be positive in these matters: hope for the best and always act, no matter how black things appear, on the assumption that they are alive and patiently waiting for help.

It is interesting how one comes to regard death when in contact with it as much as we are in mountain rescue work. Sometimes I feel that we unconsciously develop an almost dog-like attitude. Having used rescue dogs for years, I notice that when the animals find someone alive, they are overjoyed and jump around barking and wagging their tails. However, when it is a corpse that is located, the dogs show little interest. Then they see the human body as just another hunk of meat, with no affinity to life. When taking a fatality off the mountain, I, for one, don't think of him or her as anything other than a dead body. Life has gone and you are left with a redundant vehicle, which of course must be disposed of in the approved manner.

Happily, Fiona and Guy, despite the despondency they felt during that long night, were still alive and, if not kicking, were determined to get mobile and make a further effort at extricating themselves from their predicament.

What is most amazing, apart from the fact that they managed to get safely down that rock-festooned slope the previous evening, is that after they did, they started to climb another mountain – not Meall a' Bhuiridh, as they thought, but Sron na Creise. It was on the slopes of this that they had built their lean-to. They had been 180 degrees out in their direction of travel.

Fiona graphically described the morning after the long night:

"At first light, the snow and wind stopped and there was a red sky above, but despite this shepherd's warning we were full of hope and felt in our cold bones that we were going to make it to safety.

"At about 6.00 a.m. we started to climb upwards again [towards the summit of Sron na Creise] but the weather rapidly deteriorated as we struggled through the deep snow. After about three hours it became impossible to stand against that terrible wind on such a sheer slope and the snow was now waist-deep. Our legs protested; we were completely exhausted.

"We decided to traverse across the mountainside, hoping that the wind would ease and enable us to reach the next glen. In a further hour, we gained a plateau. Visibility was nil and the wind had reached such a pitch that it drove particles of snow into our faces. Guy's goggles had completely iced over so that he couldn't see through the lenses and beneath his eyelashes had bonded with ice. We now feared the worst, our earlier hopes of making it back to safety were dashed once more. We lay down, thinking this wind must be a prolonged gust, it just must ease off – it must, but it didn't. It just kept screaming over us, blowing particles of spindrift-like shot across the slope. We managed to crawl lower to a point where it wasn't quite so intense."

It must have been about 10.00 a.m. when the two lost skiers crawled to that slightly less stormy point on the Sron na Creise upper face. Meall a' Bhuiridh was very busy that day. As well as about one thousand enjoying the pistes, some seventy rescuers were examining every unusual shape and form on the wind-blasted snow slopes.

Working together on the rescue now were the official team members of RAF Leuchars, the Lochaber Mountain Rescue Team, the Search and Rescue Dog Association, White Corries ski patrol, the Glencoe Mountain Rescue Team and several casual volunteers. David Cooper from Glencoe was again back in the Cam Glen with Walter Elliot and Brian Gallacher, the Police dog handler, as were Chris Warrance and Bruce Handcock, both Met men and keen climbers. Dougie, the barman, was also in this assorted group. With the exception of the ski patrol and the casual volunteers, every team member had avalanche bleepers switched on and I can't recollect a time when there were so many reports of avalanches. The whole mountain seemed to be draped with deep snow, awaiting the slightest trigger to set it into destructive motion. The ski rescuers off the piste were finding it equally bad. It is often the case when traversing a critical snow slope, that the person on foot has less chance of starting an avalanche than the skier whose ski edges continuously break the surface tension of the snow. Someone on foot leaves a bridge between the steps and some anchorage.

Of course, it wasn't just Meall a' Bhuiridh that was wanting to shed its white cloak that day. Throughout the Western Highlands all the snow-covered peaks were in an equally bad state, but, fortunately, most climbers, more sensible than we rescuers, remained with their climbing boots firmly planted on pub floors.

I had asked Willie Elliot to take up his post again down at the Glen Etive turn-off as we had to keep in constant touch with those in the Cam Glen. Now we had full radio contact with every party on the hill, essential in case any were avalanched. The RAF Land-Rover had established a radio link on the old military road, near Ba Cottage, and to the north Stuart Obree maintained his vigil in the drifts by the side of the A82. There was still no word of the helicopter but conditions were so bad above 3000 feet that I was doubtful if it could have flown. Later it was to prove me wrong.

We had a good operation, despite the appalling conditions up top. The mountain and the surrounding glens and corries were being systematically combed and criss-crossed by the rescue skiers. Most of the Glencoe team were concentrated in the Cam Glen region with the exception of some of the skiers. A large party with John Grieve were doing a sweep across the skier-hungry east side of the glen, having gone up earlier via the Plateau. It was here that Alan Thomson and the other skiers had split off as had Davy Gunn and Bob Hamilton, who were going from the top of the mountain across the summit ridge to the T junction with the Sron na Creise-Clach Leathad ridge. Other groups, mainly from Lochaber and some of the RAF, were working beyond here in the far corries.

A string of invective from Davy Gunn presaged his message saying that he had just started a slab avalanche, but was all right. Walter told me over the RT that they were the worst conditions he had ever seen. Denis Barclay, shattered with jet lag, but still forcing himself upwards, reported snow that was head-deep in places. It was so bad in the Cam Glen that Brian Gallacher had to carry his rescue dog. It just couldn't make headway through the unstable powder.

Reports and requests for further search areas kept coming over the base truck radio. Also the three links, on two separate frequencies, were relaying progress back to base on other fronts. There was a message from Leuchars radio operator to say that the helicopter was now operational and would be with us within one hour. Some of the Lochaber team were waiting at base to be flown anywhere where they might be required should we locate Fiona and Guy.

With the search extending into the second day, Eric Moss, as self-appointed Orderly Mess Officer, had taken the precaution to make soup. Suspicious of the merits of vacuum flasks, he had constructed a hay box – a device put to good use on the plains of India during his military campaigns. In this snug manger awaited the team's soup, ready to succour the hungry coming off the hill and, I discovered, for the sustenance of the base controller. Despite my protests that I didn't normally have lunch and that I had a thermos of coffee with me, I was handed a large dixie of the undoubtedly excellent fare.

"Take this," Eric glared at me, probably thinking that I looked undernourished. "It's good for you."

I noticed that, with the addition of hay flotsam, the soup was not low in fibrous content.

"Er, thanks, Eric, I'll have it shortly," I said as graciously as possible, putting it beside the base station radio.

At the first opportunity when Eric was otherwise engaged, I quickly poured it out of the truck window, not realising that Peter Weir had placed the rescue equipment directly below. This same 'gardyloo' operation was repeated by others in the team, unaware of my pioneering gesture. All of this was much to Peter's disgust when he had to reload the broth-encrusted gear into the Land-Rover at the end of the day.

Meanwhile, over the radio, Alan Thomson and Peter Weir reported seeing what looked like a ski, high on the Meall a' Bhuiridh slopes of the Cam Glen, but Jack Williamson of the ski patrol cut in on a radio to say they had found an old ski on that slope previously. In fact, when Alan and Peter skied down to it their ski proved to be a plank of wood.

Jimmy Simpson, the Police dog handler, had set off earlier with Walter Elliot and three of the casual rescuers, the two Met men, Chris and Bruce, and Doug the barman. As Walter wryly put it, "They latched on to me thinking perhaps they had more chance of survival with one of the veterans of the team . . ."

The Wessex, which had been grounded at Rannoch, was now in radio contact. I was speaking to the 'driver', Steve Murkin, who had been on the No 6 Gully avalanche the previous day. With him was our old friend, navigator John O'Neill and winchman, Bob Danes. Steve's report of the start of activity runs thus: "Weather again bad, with strong south-westerly winds gusting to forty knots occasional heavy snow showers and low cloud. Our delay due to overnight snow accumulation and icing on aircraft. On scene at 1100 hours. Both casualties located by mountain rescue team just as R34 arrived on location."

Fiona and Guy, who were still at their last-mentioned, not-so-windy position, saw, as Fiona put it, "an opportunity to traverse across the face. In order to separate my skis, I removed a glove, and my fingers immediately stuck to the metal of the buckle; it felt as if they had just touched a hot stove. I then had great difficulty in forcing a numbed hand into my glove, but managed to do this by Guy holding the cuff in his teeth. We then tried repeatedly to step into our skis, but the drifting snow, which spilled across the surface like white foam, smothered the bindings. When standing upright, the wind still proved too strong for us. There was nothing for it but to carry our skis again. After a few paces, the sheer force of the wind blew me into the snow once more. This time the surface gave way, then I was falling. I heard Guy call, 'Dig in your toes.' Obediently I did so and immediately flipped over backwards."

When Paul Williams heard the cry from the face of Sron na Creise he looked up and saw "a pink thing coming down in an avalanche. I gave a yell to the others." The eyes of about ten of the team swung up the steep snow slopes of the mountain opposite and watched, fascinated, as Fiona plunged. Even David Cooper, who was having a pee to leeward, turned and he, too, saw the strange pink psychedelic apparition descending in the seething mass of snow. The lads didn't actually know that it was Fiona that was falling. Some of the team thought at first that it was one of our own party.

Fiona has the memory of that avalanche firmly implanted in her mind. She will, no doubt, always remember it.

"I was sliding fast, and as I saw the rocks coming towards me, I thought, I'm certain to die, but at least I won't be cold any more. I covered my face with my hands and arms and hit one rock after another. Somehow, I managed to stay close to the surface. Then, all at once, I had stopped falling, and landed in a crouching position, with one knee deeply imbedded in the snow. Now the tail-end of the avalanche caught me up and buried me, but I was still alive! Alive after falling

500 feet! As I dug myself out I turned and called to Guy.
I didn't hear him answer, but from across the glen I heard a
'Hello!'"

Her first reaction was that this was some skier calling a
friend, so she shouted, "Help!"

The answer came back, "Help is on the way."

Her relief was indescribable.

Ours was too. We had begun to lose hope of ever finding
her and Guy, but this made it all worthwhile. It was wonder-
ful to find them alive, as we dislike our too-frequent role of
mountain undertakers.

Will and Alan Thomson were high up across the valley.
They, too, had seen the 'tumbling pink thing', and took off
down the face on their skis, Will in the lead. John Grieve
and John Hardie were at about the same level as Fiona
across the glen when they heard Paul's shout and saw Fiona
fall. Guy had started to move down, sliding on his bottom,
when he heard a call from one of the team far below. "Get
to those rocks and stay there." Paul and company reached
Fiona in minutes.

At the same time Walter and his casual band had been
making their way up the left-hand side of the glen. They
were all scared of the conditions; it was like trudging across a
minefield, where at any minute all hell could break loose.

"Watch it, lads," Walter said, "keep in single file and
we'll try and follow the rocks as much as possible, but we'd
better get out of here ruddy quick."

They had just got across a snow-topped stream bed and
had gained the dubious security of rocks on the other side,
when, as Walter described it: "There was this deep boom.
We saw a crack appear just below us, across the snow. Then
from above, which may have been where the noise actually
came from, we watched as the whole head wall of the corrie
fell from a fracture line a short way down from the crest."

Will and Alan Thomson had, a few minutes before, skied
across the bottom of this slope. Now thousands of tons of

snow and ice blocks crashed down. It was probably the biggest avalanche ever witnessed in Glencoe and as it thundered down, a party of rescuers, RAF I think, were traversing the col above, but they were safe.

The radio frequencies were now overworked with a series of calls, and we relayed a map-reference for Fiona's position to John O'Neill in the Wessex. Paul Williams describes reaching her in the avalanche tip.

"I took off my jacket and gave it to her for she was desperately cold. David gave her his gloves. Her own looked as if they were made of sheet steel. John Grieve told me to climb up to the bloke, so I cramponed up to Guy. The snow was hard in the avalanche path. He didn't know if Fiona was dead or alive until I reached him."

John Grieve was now in direct radio contact with the helicopter and, after going towards another party by mistake, they zeroed in on the rescuers and Fiona. Steve describes the sequence of events from the air.

"I made several attempts to get the winchman on to the slope, but turbulence, downdraughting, a lowering cloudbase and a temperature below freezing made things extremely difficult. White-out was another problem, encountered whenever we came to the hover. Eventually we flew to the car park and offloaded excess kit not required for the rescue, took the rope from the Police Sergeant and returned to the accident scene and lowered the winchman down to the MR team and casualty."

When the first rescue attempt by the helicopter failed, Will and John Grieve carried Fiona further down the slope. Winchman Bob Danes was then lowered just downhill from this new location. Bob, not being a mountaineer, didn't like what he saw.

"Look, you guys," he greeted them, "I hate heights and don't like mountains."

Someone remarked, "Aye, then yer in the wrong place, Jimmy." But Bob, despite his 'dislikes', made it up the slope to Fiona. With the Wessex bouncing about in the turbulent air space above, Fiona was quickly prepared for the winching operation and the helicopter came back in and hovered. The winch strop was put over her head and shoulders and tightened under her arms. With Bob holding her secure, they were then both winched into the aircraft. It turned and dipped down towards the Moor of Rannoch, then in a wide semi-circle came round to the car park where Fiona was quickly bundled into the warmth of the Police Range Rover and given tea and soup.

The Wessex took off again, this time to collect Guy. The boys had been busy lowering him slowly down the slope which Fiona had descended with such alacrity a short time before. As the Wessex re-entered the Cam Glen the cloud had lowered further with the weather definitely worsening. John contacted the Wessex on the walkie-talkie.

"Can you give us ten minutes, John? It's taking some time to get the boyfriend down."

The Wessex filled in the time by ferrying down a very willing Alan and Will Thomson who were laden with their skis, though there was no hope of the whole team being shuttled back in the prevailing conditions.

Guy and Bob were eventually hoisted aboard as the big yellow machine hovered in the flank of an advancing snowstorm. It was the final operation of a very successful day.